# THE LITERARY REVIEW

SUMMER 2010
VOL.53 / NO.4

AN INTERNATIONAL
JOURNAL OF
CONTEMPORARY
WRITING

PUBLISHED QUARTERLY
SINCE 1957
BY FAIRLEIGH DICKINSON
UNIVERSITY

285 MADISON AVENUE
MADISON, NJ 07940

THELITERARYREVIEW.ORG

All correspondence should be addressed to *The Literary Review*, USPS (587780), 285 Madison Avenue, Madison, NJ 07940 USA. Telephone: (973) 443-8564. Email: info@theliteraryreview.org. Web: theliteraryreview.org. Periodical postage paid at Madison, NJ 07940 and at additional mailing offices. Subscription copies not received will be replaced without charge only if claimed within three months (six months outside US) from original date of mailing. Postmaster, send address changes to *The Literary Review*, 285 Madison Avenue, Madison, NJ 07940.

Manuscripts are read September through May. We only consider online submissions of poetry, fiction and creative non-fiction. For more information go to theliteraryreview.org/submit.html.

SUBSCRIPTIONS
One year: $24 domestic, $32 international; Two year: $36 domestic, $45 international. Single issues: $8 domestic or international.
Visa, MasterCard and American Express are accepted.

*The Literary Review* is a member of CLMP and CELJ. It is indexed in Humanities International Complete, Arts and Humanities Citation Index, MLA International Bibliography, Index of American Periodical Verse, Annual Index of Poetry in Periodicals, and the Literary Criticism Register. Microfilm is available from National Archive Publishing Company, P.O. Box 998, Ann Arbor, MI 48106. Full text electronic archives of *The Literary Review* are available through EBSCO Publishing by arrange-ment. The full text of *The Literary Review* is also available in the electronic versions of the Humanities Index from the H.W. Wilson Company, 950 University Avenue, Bronx, NY 10452. Selections from *The Literary Review* are available electronically through ProQuest LLC, 789 East Eisenhower Parkway, P.O. Box 1346, Ann Arbor, Mich., 48106-1346. Visit proquest.com or call (800) 521-0600.

PRINTING BY WESTCAN PRINTING GROUP
78 HUTCHINGS STREET, WINNIPEG, MB R2X 3B1, CANADA

COPYRIGHT ©2010
FAIRLEIGH DICKINSON UNIVERSITY
A QUARTERLY PUBLICATION
PRINTED IN CANADA

ISBN: 978-0-9841607-6-1  0-9841607-6-0

68–74: Eamon Grennan's "Conflagration Revisited" and "Going Back" are part of the col-lection *Out of Sight: New and Collected Poems*, Graywolf Press. They appear here with the permission of the author.

# TLR

**THE WORST TEAM MONEY COULD BUY**

**SUMMER 2010**

*The Worst Team Money Could Buy* is a book by Bob Klapisch and John Harper, about the Mets 1992 season from hell, that I didn't read. But I loved the title. It seems to encompass everything social, flawed, and fatal. And baseball after all is such a famously literary subject I had even assumed when we first planned this issue that it would be full to the brim with . . . baseball. Sadly, that's not how it played out. Instead, we kept finding stories and poems that seemed to be about dreadful teams, vexed efforts, and impossible odds. Each one of these exquisitely hapless tales drew us further into a purely metaphysical interpretation of our theme.

And so we have here a fifth-generation epistolary featuring anorexia, illiteracy, and email spam. An essay about a little girl getting fitted for a prosthesis. A cultural identity tale about Buffalo wings and Vietnam. A drunk who witnesses spontaneous combustion in a bar. An amazing cycle of debut poems about child abuse. Some aphorisms—not necessarily to live by. And more. Most of this Sturm und Drang is complimented by unaccountable resiliency. The stakes are emphatically awful and the characters, or their words, their innovations, or their voices are collectively, even fearsomely, tough. For which I would describe this issue as miserably peppy.

No. We didn't forget the economy—the elephant in the room. Because money money money seems to be the last thing that makes literature go round, even though in real life for so many of us finances are consuming our every anxiety. We asked several eminent writers to tell us where money fits into their literary life—because it must, mustn't it? No matter the odds, if you're doing literature, you've taken a critical step away from real life. It has to be about the game. Not the box scores.

Oh dear. I feel as if I should rouse a cheer for the underdogs.

But I'd rather read. —*Minna Proctor*

## COVER ARTIST

SIMEN JOHAN
UNTITLED #118, 2003
FROM THE SERIES *BREEDING GROUND*
DIGITAL C-PRINT

Many years ago, when my son was small, he asked me to remove all of the artwork and stuffed toys from his room that contained eyes—these things, he explained to me, were looking at him, especially in that half-grey twilight, where prowled all manner of boogiemen and under-bed monsters. It was an opportunity to see, through my child's eyes, that perceptual reality where the once obvious and benign becomes malevolent and dangerous (apologies to Winnie-the-Pooh). The work of Norwegian photographer Simen Johan reminds me with a startle of that eyeballs-in-the-closet era.

The photograph on our cover, "Untitled #118, 2003," from the series *Breeding Ground*, features an army (or is it an audience?) of snow figures, a post-apocalyptic scene of subtle, icy malevolence. Much of Johan's work from this period is dark, lyrical and generally uncomfortably cathartic. His camera functions as the painter's brush and author's words, giving us a series of composed allegories using staged, natural and digitally manipulated

© SIMEN JOHAN, COURTESY YOSSI MILO GALLERY, NEW YORK

elements. There are shadowy forest scenes, bejeweled spider webs, animals; often anthropomorphized, and interior scenes that remind one of off-beat illustrations for the Brothers Grimm. In addition to the constructed images in his photographs, Johan has added sculpture, no less evocative, to his latest exhibitions at the Yossi Milo Gallery in New York.

In a 2007 interview with *Big Magazine*, Johan commented, "I saw that we construct meaning by necessity, allowing fantasy to shape our experience of reality." And indeed, experiencing Johan's art is a glorious, if somewhat disturbing adventure into fantasy, alternate reality and the manipulation of perception, which leaves me sometimes smiling and sometimes rubbing the goose bumps on my arms. —*Jody Handerson*

# Contents

# James Richardson
# Even More Aphorisms and Ten-Second Essays from Vectors 3.0

1.

If you can't take the first step, take the second.

2.

Experience afraid of its innocence is useless: no one is rich who cannot give his riches away.

3.

My mistakes are not mine, but they are embarrassing because you might mistake them for my sins, which are.

4.

Sophistication is upscale conformity.

5.

The days are in order, the months, the seasons, the years. But the weeks are work. They have no names; they repeat.

6.

Too much apology doubles the offense.

7.

Hard disk: the letter I remembered as embarrassing is OK after all. I must have revised it just before sending. I never confuse what I dreamed with what I actually did, but this is different: which *draft* am I?

8.

What is more yours than what always holds you back?

9.

Few plans survive their first success, which suggests they were less about their goals than about the possibility of a little success.

10.

The heart is a small, cracked cup, easy to fill, impossible to keep full.

11.

How proud we are of our multitasking. What is Life but something to get off our desks, cross off our lists?

12.

The reader lives faster than life, the writer lives slower.

13.

I need someone above me—the Committee, the Law, Money, Time—to be able to say No. Sad my lack of integrity, though I suppose it would be sadder to need them to say Yes.

14.

Self-sufficiency clings . . . to itself.

15.

If you do more than your share you'd better want to: otherwise you're paying yourself in a currency recognized nowhere else.

16.

Beware speaking of The Rich as if they were someone else.

17.

We've learned to wonder which neutralizes truth more effectively, the tyranny's censorship or the democracy's ten thousand media outlets. In the former truth is too costly, in the latter there's no market for it. In Freud the facts get around the censor in the metaphors of dreams, in Shelley we live in a dream of overfamiliarity and dead metaphor that only the poet can revivify. Does repetition emphasize or hypnotize? Which is clearer, what we see or what we don't see. Are we new or old? Do we love hate or hate love?

18.

You have two kinds of secrets. The ones only you know. The ones only you don't.

19.

The peril of arguing with you is forgetting to argue with myself. Don't make me convince you: I don't want to believe that much.

20.

Tyranny and fantasy both like to write everyone else's lines.

21.

Roadkill. Something eats the eyes first, starved for . . . what?

22.

As a couple they are salt of the earth, sodium chloride. As single elements, she was a poisonous gas and he a soft and desperate metal, turning even water into roil and flame.

23.

Don't touch, don't stare. But no one minds how hard you listen.

24.

That book, that woman, life: now that I understand them a little I realize there was something I understood better when they baffled and scared me.


25.

Nostalgia for a Lost Love. At a certain distance the parts of you and her that could never love each other become invisible, which is how you got into that whole mess in the first place.


26.

Freedom has just escaped. Peace has forgotten. Boredom is pounding on the prison gates to be let back in.


27.

It is with poetry as with love: forcing yourself is useless, you have to want to. Yet how tiresome and ungenerous is the one sprawled among flowers waiting for his impulse. There's such a thing as knowing how to make yourself want to.


28.

I'm forced to admit I'm second rate: I don't have the genius's certainty about who he is. And when I talk myself into that certainty? I'm third rate.

29.

Solitude: that home water whose sweetness you taste only when you've been someone else too long.

30.

It is the empty seats that listen most raptly.

31.

No one in human history has ever written exactly this sentence. Or anyway these two.

32.

Sure, no one's listening, English will die in a hundred years, and the far future is stones and rays. But here's the thing, you Others, you Years to Come: you do not exist.

# M.A. Melnick
# Obediently Yours

From: PLAFORGE@moseycommunitylibrary.org
To: Jesus
Sent: Thursday, November 02, 2006 5:32 PM
Subject: Re: Viagra SoftTabs here

Dear Jesus,

I always believed that you would call on me. Back since I was a kid sitting next to mom and Joe on Sundays. While all else were singing, I was picturing you, flowing down and forgiving me for not doing hymns. Or better even making my voice stop cracking so as I could. I don't crack so now, but I still don't much sing. But that you know, right? Cause you know everything. So what do I tell? I might ask your pardon on account of not believing it when I first got your e-mail. And for asking Ms. Sandish who runs this place if a person could expect such a thing when they first come on the line. I figured she knows, but she kept shaking her head, in that confused way she has a habit of whenever I ask her anything, saying, polite as she always is, "I don't quite understand what it is that you are referring to." I did try to tell it to her again, but she just kept shaking her head.

Yours is the first e-mail I have ever written. Pastor Stevens said at church that us being his young forward thinking flock should take part of this Internet here at the library, cause we can reach many people with your good word. So, as you must be in knowledge of, I come to sign on everyday for almost two months. But until this day I had none else to write to.

I will surely talk over your offer to Albert as soon as I get home, and will stop back in tomorrow after work so as I'll have something better to tell.

Joyfully yours,
Parry LaForge

From: PLAFORGE@moseycommunitylibrary.org
To: Jesus
Sent: Friday, November 03, 2006 5:43 PM
Subject: Re: Viagra SoftTabs here

Dearest Jesus,

Here I am as I said I would. I found your offer extremely good. I don't know much about the price for Viagra but am sure that yours is as you say the very best. I spoke to Albert about it straight away after dinner last night, but he says there is nothing wrong with his equipment. He does admit his lack of initiative lately, but says that it is on account of the pounds I put on since our wedding. He notes that the women in my issues of It Magazine, which he takes with him to study in the bathroom, still allow his equipment to work alright and if I would look more like them, his initiative would most surely return.

Thankfully yours,
Parry LaForge

From: PLAFORGE@moseycommunitylibrary.org
To: Jesus
Sent: Monday, November 13, 2006 5:24 PM
Subject: Re: Skinny is in - are you ?

---

Dear Jesus,

Thank you for writing again. I assuredly understand that it has taken this long your being busy and such, and I feel truly blessed that you are thinking of me at all. The Ephedra sounds very luring. It's a real comfort to know that in case I need it, it is back on the market and legal when purchased from your specific pharmacy. But I think I am making progress. Albert has been very supportive. Every morning he stands with me at the mirror and circles the places with a red marker where he is sure I was not previously fat. This gives me something to recall all day while working at the store. Whenever I feel like eating and catch myself forgetting the plan, I go into the ladies' and lift up my shirt to remind me. I have found that after the first week you stop feeling starving as much and one pack of tic-tacs spaced out just so can take you through a whole day. I have lost 7 pounds already and Albert says his equipment is starting to respond again, but he will not partake with me until I reach my goal, on account it might prohabitate my progress.

Gratefully yours,
Parry LaForge


From: PLAFORGE@moseycommunitylibrary.org
To: Jesus
Sent: Monday, November 20, 2006 7:04 PM
Subject: Re: Skinny is in - are you ?

---

Dear Jesus,

I thought I would write again to tell you that Pastor Stevens has taken notice of our work and has gone to say that I have been looking very sevelt. I confessed to him that I had been in touch with you and that you have been a comfort, but that I hadn't heard from you again at all this week. He said that he of course speaks with you everyday, but that there are times when ones like me must be patient with your responses, as you have very important concerns to contend with, and that the thing to focus on was that you made your desires for me apparent. I did tell him it was Albert who had first desired for me to not to be fat, but he said that I should know that Albert was just a vessel, and it was you who really showed the way and gave me the spirit to do this. So if I haven't already said so, I am truly grateful for your guidance and look to hear from you soon.

I also confessed to Pastor Stevens that since I've been writing to you, an accurance has arrived. I started to be getting emails from others tempting to lure me from you using lower prices and free shipping. He explained to me that it is how Satan works and that I must fight it to get your message out. Since then I wrote every single one so far to proclaim that I will never buy from anyone but you, but after each time so many more come, and Albert is starting to wonder that I am getting home so late after work.

Faithfully yours,
Parry LaForge


From: PLAFORGE@moseycommunitylibrary.org
To: Jesus
Sent: Monday, December 4, 2006 8:34 AM
Subject: Re: You are nominated for mba- Bachelors, Masters or even a Doctorate

---

Dear Jesus,

I'm sorry that I didn't reply to you faster. Specially since I'd been coming before and after work now on account of having to reply to the other emailers with your message.

I wanted to respectfully wonder over your suggestion at getting my bachelors degree diploma online from the fine establishment that you spoke of. When I came on my way to work last Friday to tell you, they had the room closed down for a leak. For a few days there I was fearful at the thought that I wouldn't write to you anymore, but all is well and I am here again.

I am sad to say that Albert doesn't share your idear in regards to a education. He says that excepting with him, I have never been good around smart people. And that while I did some Bs at Mosley High, since he didn't go to college or except with Pastor Stevens or Dr. Dewitt did anyone we know, any more talk about it would make him think that I thought I was somehow better than all them. Of course I never would think like that anyhow, but he felt the need to point out the many occasions when I was not always driving on the right side of smart. This made me sad. I told him that you must already know all that and still you offered me this. But at the word of you he just screwed up his face at me and asked about dinner, then turned the TV up so as not to hear me no more.

I went back to the library and printed out your letters in order to prove it, but then thought it might be another show of pride, and it might make him to take your name in vain as I shamefully admit he sometimes does. So I hid them away with my feminine things where he will surely not go.

I figure though maybe it is true. As he says a degree wouldn't do much for me as there is no real promotion at Stan's to be gotten with college. And Albert said that if we ever had that kind of extra money, he would get us a boat to bring to the lake, as that would be a lot more fun.

Respectfully yours,
Parry LaForge

From: PLAFORGE@moseycommunitylibrary.org
To: Jesus
Sent: Friday, December 15, 2006 8:54 AM
Subject: Re: Make her scream with joy- Girls love men with big assets

---

Dear Jesus,

It is awful kind of you to be thinking of my happiness and such things, but Albert would take offense if I were to talk of his size of length. He says I am doing real good on my diet. I have now lost 18 pounds and he is so proud of me that he asks me to stop by the shop at lunch so that he can show me off to Jeffers and Coops and the rest. He took a picture of Kate Moss that he had ripped out of my magazine (the one where she is naked holding the camera) and holds it up next to me and says very soon I will be just as skinny as she is. And his equipment is working all the time now. Never seems to stop. Unfortunately I am sad to say that when I ask if we then now can have the baby he says only when he believes me that I won't just use it as a cause to be fat again. I promised and promised but he won't believe me. But what I was thinking might be if you could send me the type of female Viagra pill, I don't know what they are named, but I've heard that they exist.

Sincerely yours,
Parry Laforge


From: PLAFORGE@moseycommunitylibrary.org
To: Jesus
Sent: Monday, December 18, 2006 8:04 PM
Subject: Re: pharmacy USA Pharmacy Message 1561774

---

Dear Jesus,

Actually, I need the opposite. I am drinking cup and cup of coffee, but it doesn't even seem to help. Stan says he's giving me the front counter at the store permanently. Angy was really upset on account of her being there so much longer than me, but

Stan says it's just jealousy, that all the girls are jealous of me now and not to pay a mind to it cause I got the front counter because I had earned it. I said that I felt bad and didn't want her mad at me, and had no problem working the appliance section like last year. He just said Christmas season is all about attracting customers and he wants the prettiest girl near the big tree.

Valerie asked what I was using so that she could do it too, cause she hasn't had a lot of luck lately. I told her that she was pretty just the way she was, but she didn't want to listen. So I told her about the tic-tacs, and the marker, and that I'd started talking to you. She said she couldn't imagine that ever being enough to stop her from eating. I told her how after a while you just get sick at the thought of food. Then I thought going to Pastor Stevens might give her the inspiration. I did not come forth to give her your private address. But she sure seems to need help and so if I could ask maybe you could write to her too.

As for me, I do get dizzy an awful lot and as I say am tired always now, but everytime I complain I think of that poor man in Uzbekistan who needs that surgery but his millions are all temporarily tied up, and the American lady stuck in that hotel in Africa who can't come home until she can pay off her bill or the prince from Dubai who needs to escape, all who wrote to me needing help, and so I feel all wrong about complaining. I tried to help, I went to bring my jelly jar that I was saving all the quarters in since I was 7, thinking I could bring it all to the western union like they asked. But Albert stopped me when he saw me doing it and took it away from me, saying he counted upon it being there to put into the slots when he and the guys headed out to play pool. And he keeps asking what is wrong with me and says he's starting to have a thought that maybe there is some other man on my brain. He says now that I have lost the weight and have all these thoughts of college in my head, that I think I am too good for him. It's true what he says about men now pawing around, but I'm not lying when I say about how I am not the littlest bit interested, not the least bit interested now in anyone. So I really really do need those pills I had last discussed to you, or I can't think of what else to do.

Please help!

Hopefully yours,
Parry Laforge

From: PLAFORGE@moseycommunitylibrary.org
To: Jesus
Sent: Friday, December 29, 2006 11:04 PM
Subject: Re: Make use of every moment ? live free!

---

It's kind of spooky here at night. I thought it was on account of the lights being off, so I turned some on, but then it was even scarier. I think its all those books just looking at me. Ms. Sandish said that I was welcome to read any one so long as I made sure to put it back in the spot I found it. But I was over nervous I wouldn't remember where that was. And they are all full of stuff I don't know much of, though now I guess I could say that to just about everything. Like I didn't even know before Ms. Sandish brought the bed stuff up for me that there was a shelter down in the basement. I never even would have thought of someone bombing our own Mosley, PA, but then again maybe no one else did neither cause the blanket and pillows is a bit musty like it's been down there for a real long time. I mean no disrespect about that, it was real kind of Ms. Sandish to offer it after I confessed about having nowheres else to go, and being against the rules, I pray she doesn't get in trouble for letting me stay the night.

Its all been mostly like a dream almost. Since being at the hospital I can't put my finger on things. That first day I was brought in after passing out at Stan's, people were so nice. The nurse even patted my hand after sticking the tube in my arm, and told me they were gonna take good care of me. Stan had sent a get better balloon. Even Albert brought me pansies. He stayed with me a good while all the time saying he was so sorry to have allowed me to make my body so skinny. But the next morning everything was different. The new nurse that came in kept sighing after I told her I couldn't swallow all the food she gave and told me how it was an ungodly thing I had done to do this to myself. Then Albert came in yelling, waving about the printed letters of what I wrote you. He kept calling me un-American, naming you Haysoos, saying that I was cheating on him with a Mexican. He ripped those papers apart to pieces and threw it about the bed, then grabbed my pansies away, and said it was some way to appreciate all that he's done for me.

When the nice nurse came back and read my chart she said I was in some bad shape and should really be staying longer, but that on account of Alberts' insurance

I couldn't stay more than one more day. She said how now I needed to go home and be at rest for the week, and try to start to keep some food down.

I called and called for Albert to come get me, but then I had to take the taxi home. When I got there all my stuff had been tossed about the driveway, and Angy was standing in our doorway. I saw from the window Albert watching tv, but when I tried going in Angy wouldn't let me, because she said Albert wouldn't have me around no more.

It was no better at Stan's. He told me when I had been out so long, he was pressed to give my job to Angy's sister. He said he had no choice, someone had to do the work those three days. And that besides me being so thin makes people think that he isn't paying me enough to eat properly and so it gives him a bad reputation. Valerie was there, but would hardly talk to me on account of Angy saying how now I was the other woman. Though she did say how it was sort of cool that she was now the thinnest there and still could eat all she liked, because Stan told them all that to go losing all that weight like I had was unattractive.

I didn't understand about Pastor Stevens. With him speaking to you everyday I figured as much that he would know of the truth. But he kept saying that he could only help me after I was forgiven, and I could only be forgiven if I confessed. So I thought of things to confess, but he kept talking about the cheating. When I said it wasn't true, he said that's what Mom said too, just before she left Joe and run off with that paint salesman from Marietta, GA. And where is she now? Pastor Stevens wanted to know. I told how she moved again last year but didn't give her last forwarding address. He said, no, I mean where is she now? Which I didn't get, cause I just told him.

I suppose I could go and find her, but I was told I couldn't go nowheres right now on account of the sickness the special doctor there at the hospital said I had, and the treatment he said I needed to come to him every week. He is the doctor the not very nice nurse brought in after I said I couldn't eat all the food, who I thought must be not a very good one cause he was the only one not wearing a white coat. He's the one I told how you encouraged me to lose the weight and go to college. But it was only when I told of our emails that he stopped with the nodding and started to do a lot of writing in his pad. And firstly he says that he thinks I should see him once a week in his office, then he changed his mind and said three times. He also gave me a prescription for something named Risperdal, and so I was wondering if maybe your pharmacy carries it?

I don't have much in the form of money, when I went to get some from the bank, the counter lady said that earlier that day Albert had come and cleared it all out. But I do still have the credit card with his name on it that he gave for me, he said, only for dire straights, and I feel that now might be considered that, so do you think you might be able to take it?

Obediently yours,
Parry Laforge

# Mariana Toscas
# The Vestal Virgin Cornelia on Ortho Tri-Cyclin®

I have appeased my mother since the day
I found my baby teeth in her underwear drawer
wrapped in an embroidered silk handkerchief.
 *I come to Santa Maria Sopra Minerva.*
 *I come here to make my* oferta *to Mary over Minerva.*
 *I walk down via dei Fori Imperiali in my linen mini dress*
the way Cornelia did to join the lot of them,
(81 CE)—28 in the pack
standing at the Coline Gate—
waiting to see which virgin the Pontifex might have.
I wonder: Did she lick her lips, did she narrow her eyes
under her burqa? Did her nipples harden
when the Pontifex felt her breasts for firmness as a farmer feels fruit?
 O songs of the bridal ritual
 O songs of Hymen
 O *iam dicetur hymenaeus*
I'll go to church: A virgin bride: A polytheist:
Anything to see Cristo della Minerva sans fig leaf.
Anything to fill my wicker basket with a spill of coins.
Nobody will know if you dump your remains
in my *puticuli*—it's dark in here. The reservoir
of modesty has burned through its system of membranes—

to my right Mother sings the songs of Catullus
in a raspy whisper: *excitusque hilari die nuptialia concinens . . .*

*Just beat me with myrtle twigs.*

We're on our sugar pills now, but these synthetic hormones
can make you get to your knees and put your nose to the stone.
What was Cornelia hiding in the underside of her stola?
     O ethinyl estradiol
     O norgestimate
     O microcrystalline cellulose and pregelatinized corn starch
"I seize you, beloved." We'll launch an asynchronous orgy
in Minerva's parlor. How many 78 rpm records can I play
with each steel needle? The Victrola diaphragm vibrates:

*Uoce carmina tinnula pelle humum pedibus manu pineam quate taedam . . .*

For I am to be the virgin bride.
For I am to be the bride of Vesta.
For I am to be the childless child.
     *In the name of the father.*
     *In the name of the father.*

# Sodomy

Before I feel you slice through me, I sleepwalk
from the bedroom,
step back, find my two halves running up the cellar

from the fiery mouth of the furnace, the one half
tucked into Nona's
orange flowered apron while she peels potatoes with a paring knife.

The other, younger half swaying up the road
gathering autumn leaves
in her skirt. No, she is bleeding. In the bedroom,

You guide the thing between your legs like a dousing rod
As fruit flies gather
on the underside of a lemon in a clay bowl. I wheeze.

Nona swirls camphor on my chest like silver polish
while your saliva
lathers on my ear. Downstairs, the older one winds

the grandfather clock with a mainspring crank, while
the younger girl bows
a cello in a room where it is always two o'clock.

# The Butcher's Daughter

The dark-haired girl leaves the *macelleria* for the Metro,
its door handles opening and closing like a freezer:

> *Battistini, Cornelia, Valle Aurelia—*

In a few hours, Nona will be over the stove, stirring
saffron into bouillon base with a wooden spoon.
Her mind moves to her father,
moving slowly and calmly through the herd,
trying not to kill one animal in front of the others,
then to god but not really God—moonlight flickering
neon over her knuckles—or Mary with her Cubist
nose and thin-shadowed lip. More of a daisy chain
of goddesses, entities with rippling seafoam
slips, gold-veined skin, creamy cuticles never tasked
with pulling muscle from muscle or turning intestines
inside out and scraping them with a knife.

Before she was born, Father watched while the Blackshirt
choked mother with his gold-tipped scabbard
and raped her on the butcher block. Now he only talks
of his light-haired sons, and he only slaughters

pigs: "Swine don't care if you slaughter their mate in front of
them, they'll rush over to drink the blood."

*Cipro, Ottaviano, Lepanto—*

The clay smell of toenails and of sour wool swells,
each carcass carefully aging in break dust and
epinephrine, terrified of its upright form,
its swinging arms, its hair follicles, its vertebrae
hardware, its weight.

*Spagna, Barberini, Repubblica—*

She enters late, Father turns to the window
and pretends to sleep. The wallpaper is damp
with grease and the smell of pig's feet floating
in the kettle—a thin layer of gelatin
hardening on top. Nona plays solitaire
on an uneven table until she wins.

# A Penny for a Needle

*A PENNY FOR A SPOOL OF THREAD,*
*A PENNY FOR A NEEDLE.*
*THAT'S THE WAY THE MONEY GOES,*
*POP! GOES THE WEASEL!*
*YOU MAY TRY TO SEW AND SEW*
*AND NEVER MAKE SOMETHING REGAL*
*SO ROLL IT UP AND LET IT GO*
*POP! GOES THE WEASEL!*

*I pray, dear lord I prayed,*
    I sewed
that and the other holy ghost into my boncs, thread
a net of capillaries tight as a burr inside
       my cock, but its splintering heat is cast deep
as a spell from a stolen amulet, its eye
                precise as thistle.
    There is no salve
for the pricked palms of desire, whose heavy finger
pads debone her soul's fish just      behind the gills;
    no psalm
for her clit quivering like a lone prayer
bead on a line, red & raw   between my thumb;
    no hymn
sweeter than that gypsy ribbon      pulled from the song
in her throat;
    no hook & eye closure between her thighs

               to stop me

from mock humming her blood
        line through my teeth, pulling bones from the melody
in her ear with my tongue, dancing
        in the distilled vapor of her throat
of salt, spitting her          into a thimble of mucus.

*I pray, dear lord I prayed,*

                        I'll hold
                                onto that wild fuck like a fetus in a water jar.

# Girls Like Us

I tell you this—
when he died, what I noticed first
was his tongue: longer than it seemed
and dirtier, like the unseen part
of a clogged drain stop.
I tell you this—
I took his fist once more, savored
his spit in my mouth as a last supper
of sorts, made sure I got my fill
of his belt on my back, I even
shed a tear when he forced me on my knees.
I tell you this—
I couldn't look away while he had
his way. Now, his mottled blue
face bores me. I boiled clear broth
and drank it from a flowered mug
while he decayed—tousled his hair,
put my mouth to his ear and whispered
*I'd rather hate.*
        I tell you this—
I had to put it to an end,
these things aren't healthy.

Each time his hand encircled my neck
I sunk into the slump of ecstasy,
deeper and deeper into the suck
of nonentity. I—the victim?
Deep inside, girls like us
like it when it hurts.
I tell you this—
someday, I'll have a gentleman
go gentle with me
and I'll pretend that this is what
girls like me really want
deep inside.
I tell you this—
I'll remember most
how my cunt twitched
as I stood murmuring in some
dead tongue over his body.

# Jason Lee Brown
# Big Cowboy

FOR JAY PREFONTAINE, WRITING PARTNER, CO-EDITOR, AND FRIEND (1963–2010)

The Festival of the Steel Phallus came on the first Sunday of April, during the precious two weeks when the cherry blossoms bloomed. Near the shrine, three young women pounded drums with sticks they swung fast enough to blur. The crowd, many of them European and American, had multiplied in the last hour, and Aya could barely squeeze between the men and women of all ages. She stopped next to a man wearing a traditional happi coat. The man hugged a three-foot black penis that drew a procession of festival-goers who, one by one or in groups, hugged, rubbed, or leaned against its steel for photographs and videos.

She had purposely allowed her husband to wander off long enough for him to panic, for him to know how she often felt in central Illinois. She watched Ted's every move from a few meters away, and whenever he looked for her, she hid inside the walkway of a wooden structure next to the shrine. The structure had a purple roof and postcard-size wooden plaques on every inch of the round posts and sidewalls. Aya had just bought two of the prayer plaques.

Ted paced in a small circle, as if inside an invisible cage. He'd followed her around like a huge puppy the entire trip, and she was tired of being his translator. When he rose on his tiptoes, his short red hair bobbed well above the sea of black hair. By himself, he could never figure out which trains to take back to the hotel. He was a-different-country, a-different-language lost. He had 10,000 yen in his pocket where he kept his passport and a little notepad on which Aya had written the name of their hotel and the closest train station. He would never be able to find her if she left him.

Two male flutists joined the drummers, and the amalgam of sounds echoed in her chest. She watched Ted sip sake from his masu. He stuck out, not only because of the black Harley Davidson tee shirt and pink-freckled skin, but because he looked confused, as if he didn't know how to take it all in. While he again stood on his tiptoes, a lanky European man wearing a large, strap-on penis slammed its Styrofoam head into Ted's hip, knocking him off balance and spilling sake down his arm. He straightened up ready to defend himself, but the lanky man had hopped away on an invisible stick horse with a couple of his friends, poking strangers from behind and moving on before the victims knew what had hit them. The men whooped and hollered, spreading their seed everywhere, pillaging the village.

Behind Ted, three girls in green skirts, jackets, and long white socks stood in front of the shrine's entrance. The one in the middle—with her skirt folded at the top so it rose up her thighs—tossed coins into a collection box. She pulled the middle rope, and a bell rang. With her palms together in front of her face, she bowed. Aya wondered what the girl was praying for. Had she disobeyed, lied? Was she pregnant?

She peeked around the walkway for Ted. He wasn't there. She thought she had really lost him until she saw him buying more sake at a booth right next to her. He held out 10,000 yen for a 600-yen refill, and then stuffed the change in his front jean pocket without checking to see if it was correct. Aya held an ema in each hand and rubbed her thumbs across the wooden plaques that were light as a pack of cigarettes and ran different scenarios in her head about how Ted would greet her. She imagined him hugging her without saying anything, or thanking God he found her, or simply apologizing.

"Where you been?" she said through the crowd. This was what he'd always said to her after he'd disappeared at parties where she knew no one—getting high with his friends, driving to the liquor store, talking to another girl, or whatever he was doing.

"Where've I been?" he said. He swaggered through the few people between them holding his sake like a warm cup of coffee.

"Been here the whole time," Aya said.

"Don't quote my own words back to me. I was worried about you."

"Me?" She was amazed how he tried to make it her fault, make her feel small.

"There could be a lot of freaks in this environment," he said. "And you go missing. What am I supposed to think?"

"You were missing. I was buying your ema." She handed him a prayer plaque.

"Why do we need two?" he said. "Thought we were sharing."

"Two prayers are better than one." She gave him a black marker. "Write your prayer on the back. Sign your name underneath."

The drums and flutes quickened to a crescendo that never seemed to peak. He studied the front of the ema that had an outline of the shrine with a fat red penis reaching toward the roof and a ringing bell.

"Great," he said. "Another pecker. Peckers for everyone!" He held up the ema. "Come on, people! Peckers! Sign your pecker here!"

She slapped his elbow. "Don't be disrespectful."

"Fine," he said. He signed his name under the words WANT HEALTHY BABY.

## Two prayers are better than one.

He tied his ema to the wooden pole. The structure had hundreds hanging on it, and Aya doubted her lone prayer could fight through all the others. She took back the marker, and when she stepped under the roof to write down her prayer, Ted hovered over her shoulder. The drums and flutes blurred into one until the music stopped, leaving a slight ringing in her head. On the front of her ema was Momotarō, the Peach Boy, bursting out of a giant peach, his arms spread in a V. She flipped the ema over and wrote in Japanese: STRENGTH TO LEAVE.

Aya and Ted stood next to one of the many souvenir booths featuring a seemingly endless array of phalluses: charms, stickers, lollipops, cups, canteens, chocolates, carrots. Other booths had little Buddha statues with huge erections, iron-penis neck-laces, and rubber penises that hung out of zippers. On the ground, three middle-aged men on a green tarp carved white radishes. Once in a while, a man's voice would issue a cheerful announcement over the public address system. This time it was "Sex is wonderful! Try it for fun!"

Ted sipped sake from his freshly filled masu. He preferred Budweiser, but while in Japan, he acted like a long-time connoisseur of sake. He tried the most expensive brands everywhere Aya took him, and while at the festival, he slurped down one cup after another.

"Cute," she said. She held up a penis-shaped key chain. She pulled on the testicles and the penis grew erect. She giggled and tried to hand it to him.

He squinted and waved his hand in front of his face as if shooing a fly, and if she didn't know better, she would swear he was in pain.

"Think I should buy gag gifts to send back?" She held up a family-size pack of penis lollipops. Each pack had four, two life-size ones for the grownups and two thumb-size ones for the kids. "My coworkers will think they're funny."

"Why are you even asking? You're going to buy them anyway."

He was right. It was her money. Her coworkers. Why was she asking him? He didn't even know her friends. She bought one large pink lollipop for herself and a small yellow one for Ted. She also purchased three family sets of lollipops for her coworkers. She took the heavy sack of souvenirs from the man behind the booth and reached inside for the pink and yellow lollipops. She looped the sack around her forearm, struggling to hold it and her black purse while opening her lollipop.

"A little help, please," she said.

Ted grabbed the sack from her and tucked it under his crossed arms. "You bought them. You should have to carry them."

"I bought this one for you." She held out the yellow lollipop.

"You shouldn't have wasted your money."

"I'm not wasting it." She twisted the pink lollipop on her tongue. "Mmm, it's good. Strawberry. Taste it."

"I'm not putting that thing anywhere near my mouth," he said. He stared at a man wearing a pregnant belly under a long, peach dress. "If there's really something wrong, this whole festival could be a waste of—"

"Just accuse me, if you're going to accuse me."

"It could be me," he said, quickly.

She knew he didn't believe it. He had bragged many times about his fertile Catholic family, and though he had only one brother, he had nearly thirty cousins, all of them in the same small town. And she knew she wasn't young anymore. The maturity in her skin was like an old friend whose age she recognized before the face. There was no gradual change to it; she was young months ago but now had creases and crows feet. Whatever cuteness she used to have was gone.

"Maybe it's the steroids you did for football," she said.

"Three cycles, that's it. And that was years ago."

"You won't talk about it so I wouldn't know. Would I?"

"That just leads to more questions, about ex-girlfriends, and how many of them still live in town, and I'm not getting into that again because it never ends."

All she could think about were the women Ted hadn't told her about. He'd cheated on her the same night his brother died with what he called, "Nobody, a one-nighter." Aya didn't even ask for details, at least not then. Years of fretting and paranoia had dulled her. It wasn't his cheating but that she never would have known if he hadn't been forced to tell her. "I caught something," he'd said. At first, she'd thought he meant a cold. He even cried. The next day his doctor told him he'd spread poison oak all over himself while rolling around with Nobody. When he came home, he started talking about a baby and hadn't let up. This was what broke her. This was what set all this in motion, the trip to Japan, the festival, her lying. She'd told Ted she'd stopped taking the pill months ago, but every month, she refilled her prescription.

"Look." She pointed at a group of middle-school boys in navy-blue uniforms, who were stuffing penis-shaped candies into their mouths. The boy with the long black bangs pulled out his lollipop. It was mangled into a different shape.

Ted rolled his eyes and Aya wondered what kind of child he would raise. She knew he would have his boy riding a four-wheeler to his hunting tree with his dog and rifle by age ten. He even wanted to name the first boy Ted, Jr. Ted Jr.! She did not think of these fatherly attributes as negative or insufficient. She simply thought of them as Ted. He never paid her close attention, never asked how she was doing or how she felt, never gave her hugs or kisses for no reason. But in the last few months, he'd been caring and purposely avoided arguments. His newfound niceness—the opening of doors, the fetching, the frequent calls, the gifts—stood goosebumps on the back of her neck.

"Come on, taste it," she said. She tapped his chest with the yellow lollipop and the cellophane wrapper crinkled. "I got the small one just for you."

"Funny, but still no go."

She stuck her pink lollipop in her mouth and rolled it on her tongue. She cherished his discomfort and licked the pink all over before smacking her lips.

"Stop it."

She didn't see the problem. It was a fertility festival to raise money for AIDS. She translated the yellow pamphlet that stated the festival dated back to the Edo Period and that the shrine used to be popular among prostitutes who prayed for protection against sexually transmitted diseases. When Ted told her to stop translating every single thing here, she moaned, swirled the lollipop in her mouth.

He pulled her forearm and the lollipop popped out. "It's not funny."

She wondered how long it would take before he again mentioned her converting to Catholicism. She'd refused him without discussion. Only three times in her life had she seen Ted kneel next to his bed and pray: when he thought she was pregnant in college, when his only brother died, and when he decided he wanted a baby.

"You will never see anyone here ever again," she said. "It's not like you're coming back." He walked away a few steps, waiting for her to grab his arm. "Bye-bye," she said. She headed in the opposite direction. She could barely weave through the thick crowd, but it felt good doing it.

"Where you going?"

She didn't turn back but could hear him apologizing to people. She wanted this new confidence to swell even more and develop into something sustainable, but she knew it would never survive the trip back to his hometown, where she followed him around like a pet, getting second looks everywhere she went, then smiles that seemed to say, "Oh, just Ted's Oriental wife, nothing to worry about." Or they would talk to her like a child, confusing her accent for ignorance.

The public address system announced, "Sex is wonderful! People should have more sex and make more babies!"

Aya stopped at an open area near two fifteen-foot-long wooden penises that were tied to a wooden cart at a forty-five degree angle like rockets ready to launch. People crowded around, taking photographs and videos. They laughed at friends and family members who petted or straddled them.

**When he came home, he started talking about a baby and hadn't let up. This was what broke her.**

Ted pinched her elbow and turned her around. "What's gotten into you?"

She acted surprised to see him. "Hi, there! How are you?" She lodged the lollipop in the corner of her mouth like a cigar then smiled, waiting for him to speak.

"Alright, fine, tell me what you want me to do, and I'll do it."

The lollipop between her teeth slurred her words into wet crackling sounds. "What did you expect?"

"Not this."

"Sex is wonderful!" the public address system announced. "Remember, you are all here because your parents had sex!"

An old man in a gray suit and thick black glasses sat on one of the wooden penises. He flashed a peace sign at coworkers who shot photographs. His friends gathered around the digital camera. "Ooh-ooh." Some laughed. "So, so, so, so."

Aya pulled Ted closer. "Rub it, for fertility."

Ted shook his head in disgust then stroked the light brown wood. He whispered, "Good, boy. Everything's fine, just do what they say, and it will all be over soon."

She pulled her camera from her purse. "Hop on."

The salarymen and others around them clapped and cheered him on.

"Do you want a baby or not?" she said.

His eyes widened as if she'd smacked him.

She couldn't believe she'd said it, but she wished she'd done it years ago. After they married, he wouldn't discuss having a child. The only thing he said was, "We don't have time now. We're career people." She stopped asking for a family, and after a few more years, she found herself resenting the idea of children with Ted. She'd missed her baby window, and there was nothing she could do but cut her losses.

"You asked for it," he said. He chugged some sake then handed her the masu and sack of souvenirs. He kicked his foot up and over the wooden penis. His height allowed him to stand halfway up the shaft. The salarymen told him to slide down to the base of the penis to show the length. Aya translated, and Ted slid to the bottom. The salarymen applauded and cheered.

"See, it's not so bad," she said.

"Like having sex in a crowded room," he said.

He was small on the camera's LCD screen, small enough to hold him in her hand and put in her pocket any time she pleased. She froze him in place.

"Big cowboy, big cowboy!" one of the salarymen said.

It wasn't until Ted acted like a bull rider swinging an invisible cowboy hat above his head that Aya recognized he was imitating one of his favorite movie scenes, where a cowboy rides an atomic bomb to the earth. Ted thought the black-and-white movie was hilarious, but Aya didn't pay enough attention to understand it. Ted rubbed his crotch against the wooden penis and growled. The crowd cheered louder. He raised his arms and thrust his hips until his face turned red. She took more photos.

After he hopped off, he was quiet. She gave back his masu. He stared at the sake. She'd seen this before. He was drunk and thinking too hard about things. She hooked her arm around his and pulled him away from the wooden penises and into an open area.

"Only positive memories, remember?" she said.

He gulped the last of his sake. "I should've been the one to have kids, not my brother."

Outside the Kanayama Shrine, the streets were packed with people waiting for the rest of the procession to return. Aya and Ted stood near the curb under the blooming cherry trees. The souvenir sack swung from his wrist as he sipped sake. She stared at the light pink flowers, listening to the chanting and loud music, thinking about the first day she'd met Ted, in a business class in college. She'd thought something was wrong with him because he kept smiling at her. She later learned that he smiled at everyone.

She wished the relationship would have ended with the class, wished she wouldn't have been so flattered by the first American male who showed interest in her, despite her shyness and accent. She'd planned out her life since she was nine. She'd attended her preferred schools in Kawasaki, and then moved to the States. Ted's proposal fit her life's schedule—married at age twenty-six—but she'd rearranged her happiness for him. She'd already told him they had seats several rows apart on the flight home and that he would have to board first. He would be an hour into the flight before he noticed she wasn't there.

The chant of "Dekkai-mara! Dekkai-mara!" grew louder, and when Aya looked up the street, there it was, a seven-foot pink penis named Elizabeth, bouncing up and down. Elizabeth had been mounted on a mikoshi, a portable wooden shrine carried on the shoulders of fifteen transvestites, each of whom wore a silky pink happi, a wig, and an abundance of mascara and red lipstick. Elizabeth, with a fat mushroom head and ropes that secured her testicles to the portable shrine, shook in time with the rhythmic chant. Adults swarmed around the mikoshi and held cameras, cell phones, and recorders over their heads for a better angle.

"Pink like a Pepto-Bismol bottle," Ted said. He'd drunk himself back to happy. "What are they chanting?"

Aya joined the chant. "Big Penis! Big Penis!"

He stumbled off the curb and cupped his free hand around his mouth. "Shake it, Pink! Pinky! Pink-kay!"

Elizabeth and the procession advanced down the street toward the shrine where the priests would eventually bless all three mikoshi and declare the festival a successful worship. With each breeze, the cherry blossoms showered down on the street and sidewalk where hundreds of footsteps trampled them. One landed in Aya's shirt collar, its head resting in the crook of her neck.

# Benjamin Paloff
# Identity and Difference

:: Peter Richards

Let us call our pharmaceuticals all by their courtesy names
and march out east with all the beau-less
girls who moved to town in vintage gowns and were charged
with disturbing the war to come back triumphant
to the awesomest shtetl in the world and fade
in unlamentable ways because even in the calmest seasons
deciduous fingers stir red doldrums to a breeze
and the heart buries its head
in category to please calamitous reason
which answers my aporias with a sneeze
and then my participation in civic process stuffs me
overfull with irrational exuberance and paltry gratitude
I wouldn't begrudge Thanksgiving's
food-pantry-born excuses for poultry equally overstuffed
and the pumpkin pie oversweet and not
enough and the carrots and corn by which I mean maize
all desiccated and misdirected from dualities I wouldn't dare

erase the scale of our being as seen from below
parrots or pocketbooks pickpockets porn the resurrected
dead or their dread Scottish terriers
insurrections or films I won't see colds I won't suffer
women I won't bed all whittled down into this
bin or its brother binding me to myself
or if not to my other
in the awesomest shtetl ever our culture is popular
the burden of an observational logic too great
not to ascribe to the thing observed
and the thicker the mire the wider the pit the brighter
the halo we see rung above it the lime basil in the garden
running molecules of shit so efficiently through its inscrutable
machine making of them something we are eager to put
in our mouths it is all we need for a clock around here
the clock more and more like us watching the clock
the masses more massive now stirred to a song

inside     and      out      never      wrong      nor      unright

the     whole     village     now     shooting     into     the     sky

like     there's     somebody     up     there     who     owes     us

money     and     it's     only     because     we're     living     at     the     end

of          the          Age          of          the          Book

that     I'm     home     writing     letters     to     you

my     first     my     last     and     unrequited     love     the     sea

# Difference and Repetition

:: IGA NOSZCZYK

I      see      with      the      eyes      of      a      hospital
visitor      the      second      I      give      up      my      cell      phone      I      count
the      minutes      before      I      will      leave      no      mark
o r      a      m a r k      t h a t      f a d e s
like      the      ghosts      rotting      leaves      leave      in      pavement
the      sky      so      bright      I      can      see      the      kingdom      coming
though      the      sky's      so      bright      I      can't      use      that      line      again
all      the      proper      names      dialoguing      within      me
English      into      Russian      Russian      into      Polish      as      if
by      embellishing      our      countries      of      origin      with      a      hush      or      a      yen
we      might      accurately      represent      nationality      as      if
the      easiest      way      to      surround      myself      with      animals
were      to      give      them      food      or      to      be      that      food      as      if
by      removing      myself      the      vectors      remaining      among      every      beast
and      proper      name      would      accurately      represent      both      me
and      my      absence      in      the      same      way
that      by      mapping      a      minefield      and      removing

all surface features but the positions of mines will yield a new map of no place though I find the analogy more than a little baroque when Dominick LaCapra refuses to face me at the symposium I get used to thinking his face has one ear in the middle an eye and a nose on the side like an anthropomorphized flounder of trauma his speech soft and mined with rough cavities like a goat eating an heirloom tomato the whole time he is speaking I wonder what else is there to do to the dead but speak ill all of us in our infinite parallel lives make an incredible army and you whose English is baroque in a way I wish were correct declares that LaCapra is a shit he is a total fucking shit though now that I think about it I think you are thinking of an American movie and only seeing like a hospital visitor my tendency

to read or see something that inspires me to stop
fucking around to learn the language to take up arms
knives in hand when every sound calls to mind a song
I cannot stand this one goes out
to all you umpires out there
to those who despite everything we've been through insist
on stuffing their paper towels down the toilet
to children in crowns and macramé
this one's for you Desiderio's relief of John the
Baptist as a child Max Ernst's spanking of Christ
for my own children wonderfully monstrous
in that way that drives me to prayer
you see me just that clearly
because whenever I'm given a break I promptly regift it
to the world and in the morning you greet me with my fortune
don't sleep too much you say text me

# Repetition/Fear and Trembling

:: FIRST GIRLFRIEND, NAMED JESSICA

Sleeping too much in context playing dumb and cracking wise
I cross out and revise and redoubt and remember the classes
I ditched the lockers and clockers and summertime girls
still refusing to step to the woo that I pitched
and the only beat I ever laid down
in the first grade Sonny D'Agostino
because sleeping too much I have no time
for Damon Runyon characters to identify
the aesthetic inadequacy of the ghost of the travesty
I'm watching on television
whose rectangular light reaches up toward
and is very much like the stone monolith on the moon
in 2001 despite my credentials
I believe in the occult
symbologies of the man washing water
off the stones with a garden hose
over and over again in the morning

though it is the washing not the man
or the garden I believe in
full of ghosts in the twilight
every name a convenient metaphor
for the sadness of naming plants though you can't
put a postage stamp on melancholy
or a finger on the poisonous taste in your mouth
and that would be the poison
when you have nothing
else to say tell me whom you loved that day
because if no one in New York
calls Sing Sing a prison
it's the second sing that makes it so

# M. Eileen Cronin
# The Hanger Artificial Limb Company

The leg man says I'm supposed to stand up on my new legs today; Mom says I'm going to walk to the end of the parallel bars; and I'm thinking about the metal pinchers on the leg he showed me the last time we came. Maybe I could just squiddle instead?

Now, at almost five, I'm still tilting on my knee then shoving off from my other leg to get around, and we call this squiddling. My thirteen-year-old sister, Annie, made up the word. This is what we do in our neighborhood. We make up words and nicknames, though I prefer Danny B.'s nickname for me, "Lear Dear."

Danny's skin is brown as tanned leather because he spends all summer in his swimsuit. The B. boys brag that they don't have to bathe because they swim instead. That I am someone's Dear, even a boy who hasn't bathed all summer, seems a step up from being Eileen, the squiddler. *Lear Dear*, whispers Danny. Then he curls those lips, stained blue by a Freeze Pop, as if we share a secret.

Annie, on the other hand, says squiddle with her eyes narrowed and a smirk on that mouth, set as it is to the side of her face, making the whole point seem devious. "Ska-wid-del a-long, I-lean!" she says.

Our parents scold her, though, usually they're fighting a grin when they say, "Stop it, Ann! That's so awful!"

Danny, however, has coined a cheer: "Squiddle along, Lear!"

Because he says it with pride rather than as a taunt, I've made squiddling into a sport. If I want to speed up I throw my arms into it and gallop. I brag that I can outrun Danny's dog, Topper.

The whole neighborhood is in on the sport. In my chase to keep up with a pack of roving kids, I trot over lawns and past brick-and-siding colonials. The moms glance over newspapers from their screened-in porches, the dads over the spray of hoses on steamy tar-coated driveways, and everyone cheers me on: "Squiddle along, Lear!"

Proud as I am of my speed, I know that squiddling is something people outside our neighborhood wouldn't get. I cannot squiddle into school, for example. I won't turn five until late September, so I could stay home another year, but Mom is eager to get these legs made. She wants me to stop throwing tantrums, stop wrapping my body around her ankles, and stop demanding, "Put me on that bus. I want to go to school now!"

Mom is hoping not only to send me to school but to have me *walk* into kindergarten.

So nowadays we practically live at The Hanger.

The last time we went to The Hanger the leg man said, "Let me take a look at that stump." I drew back and sucked my thumb. Then I picked at the smocking on my Polly Flinders while this ancient man ran his bony fingers over cold, wet plaster on my thigh to get a perfect mold. Mom sat beside me, her pointy elbow digging into her pregnant belly, a forgotten cigarette dangling from her hand, and her head cocked sideways with an open-mouthed stare fixed on the goop. She cannot take slime. Meanwhile the leg man, on his knees, kneaded the wet plaster up my thigh, which made me gasp and wheeze. "Can you lift that up?" he said, pointing with his chin at the hem of my dress. I turned to Mom, expecting her to slap his face, but she was still locked into that vacant stare. So I did as he asked and closed my eyes as he leveled the furthest edge of the cast.

When I looked down again, the leg man was dipping his hands into a bucket of water. Then he smoothed his wet palms along the surface, ironing out every single bump. "Gotta work fast," he said, "before it dries." In about fifteen minutes, he yanked the solid white mold from my thigh. That's when Mom snapped to attention, stamping out the now-remembered butt with its two-inch ash. In a flash, she was up on her pumps leaning forward, her dark, outstretched arms the signal for me to leap into the tent of her sleeveless shift and mount that pregnant belly. My head was foggy, haunted by those fingers on my thigh.

"Well, come on!" Mom snapped. Then she jutted out her lower lip and huffed like Lucille Ball blowing a chunk of bangs from her eyes—as if Mom's black-lacquered bangs could possibly fall.

Next she clapped her hands and shouted, "We're done!" And the leg man lifted one of his own legs from the kneeling position—the artificial one—and rested his elbow on the fake thigh while he lit his own cigarette. "For now," he said. "But we still gotta fit 'em."

I jumped and landed with a thud against Mom's stomach. I had to pull myself over her pregnant belly to coil my arms around her neck, which smashed her breasts and knocked the wind out of her. She gasped and I heard, "haaa." Then she said to the guy, "What?"

"She's gotta stand up in 'em." He said this with a cigarette clenched in his teeth. "One at a time."

"Well, of course she does!" said Mom, stomping a foot. (She watches Shirley Temple too.) "I'll be dipped. You'd think I was born yesterday. Just tell me how many more o'these we got?"

"Let's see," he said, holding out an open hand. He started with his thumb. "There's the below-knee leg for starters. Can't have her stand on the AK before she gets up on the BK. Then there's—"

"Oooh! Skip it!" said Mom. "Just call when it's time to come back. And don't leave any messages with that Jessie. She always gets 'em screwed up."

"You got a ton o'kids, ma'am. Which one's Jessie?"

**Proud as I am of my speed, I know that squiddling is something people outside our neighborhood wouldn't get.**

"The colored lady," said Mom, halfway through the door. Then she mumbled to herself, "Who-do-ya think?" I watched him from over her shoulder as we turned the corner. He had cocked his head sideways, scratching his ear with a match, confusion on his face.

So, here we are, another week, another drive across town to The Hanger. There's a red light up ahead and as usual Mom is gunning the accelerator. "I'm a nervous wreck," she says before slamming on the brakes at the last second. "What is this? Our sixth time?"

Six, seven, what do I know? I only know that we call this place The Hanger, which I suppose has something to do with the man's leg hanging in the window.

Still, sitting here at the light, I'm wishing I could be on my way to anywhere else. We're in the rundown part of Walnut Hills, not far from the mansion at DeSales Corner, where Mom lived as a baby. Now, in 1965, that house is a funeral home. Most of the others are shabby apartment buildings. This is worlds away from Finneytown, our neighborhood with its flat lawns and new houses.

We turn into a square. The oldest parts of Cincinnati have so many squares. Some are bound by fancy shops and outdoor cafés, and some are like this one: cars staggered diagonally at meters in the hub of businesses that people need but hope they won't. We are surrounded by appliance repair shops, prosthetics, funeral parlors, and everything medical. Mom's edgy because she can't find parking. "Used to be you wanted to live in Walnut Hills," she mutters. Then she yanks the wheel so hard that something screeches as she circles the hub.

I look up from my window at turrets and spires jutting from third stories. My eyes sweep down patterned brickwork to the picture windows at street level. They are now plate glass windows showcasing wheelchairs, caskets, and Alka Seltzer. Mom glides her gold, square-back Volkswagen into a metered spot. In the rearview, she checks her brown velvet eyes for smudges. She dabs at the edges of her lips for the same and runs a finger over the arch of each black eyebrow. Before she married Dad, Mom was an artist. She made pen-and-ink drawings of models wearing smart suits with berets. Dad says Mom is as pretty as Liz Taylor, and to me she is just as glamorous.

I look back at the leg dangling in The Hanger's window. Underneath it is a March of Dimes poster. Maybe a part of me will hang beside that leg in the window? Which is fine. (I secretly dream of being the March of Dimes poster child.)

The boy who is now in the poster leans into crutches, as if to struggle for every step. I'm impressed by his slicked hair and pressed suit in the black-and-white photo. I imitate the way he sets his jaw, so determined. This is a boy everyone loves, I'm sure of it. I figure that if I were the March of Dimes girl people would love me just as much. They would stand in line for a chance to lug me around. So, if all I have to do is dangle my own wooden leg in that window to get "discovered," then I might just do it.

I'm roused from this daydream when Mom plucks me from the passenger seat by the armpits and kicks the door closed. She leverages me on one pregnant hip as she struggles to find change for the meter. Her purse is almost as big as a carpet bag. I'm slipping down so I shimmy up to lodge on the upper side of her hipbone, but the baby in her belly gets in the way. I'm skidding off like a kitten clinging to a basketball. I see the shards of glass littering the curb and imagine that glass piercing my skin.

Then I remember the time Mom carried me past the man without legs, who held a tin cup under the awning of Pogue's Department Store downtown. I wonder, how does he squiddle on a street like this one?

I try to get a look at Mom's face, but she's twisted and wriggling to get at the change. That's when it occurs to me that aside from getting me into legs so that I can go to school, Mom only wants to fling me from her hip so she doesn't have to carry me anymore. She has a toddler at home already: Joe, the black-eyed-monster. Lucky for her he was running before he could crawl. He catapults to the kitchen counter and swings from the cabinets like a monkey-boy. Soon Mom will have the black-eyed-monster, a new baby, and me, not to mention the six kids who walk for themselves.

I wince at the glass and decide that I will not be thwarted by a baby ball. The deal is off, poster girl or not. I will not be a part of this Hanger experiment. Even the doctors aren't sure I will be able to walk in those legs. Why should I try? Instead, I could sit back and let Mom lug me around for life. Then I'll have her all to myself. So, no, she will not get me off of this hip, no matter how big her baby ball grows.

Mom is now reaching into her handbag, balancing it on her thigh as I cling for life. This is when I tell her, "I'm not doin' it. I'm not goin' in there!" The purse, which is flung open with Mom's hand digging into the wallet for change, is balanced, just barely, on her thigh. She isn't having any of my fuss. So I dig my fingers into her chest and shove away from her, squirming as I do it. She has to hold up a leg to keep me from falling. She's hopping around on one leg to keep me from toppling onto a sidewalk of broken glass, or to keep from spilling her purse into the gutter, or to keep us both from going down in a suicidal sprawl over that broken bottle. "Stop it!" she snarls, and I'm thinking, "Who's sorry now?" We dip, we twirl, the glass pointing back at us from this angle and that, until I lose my nerve.

And we both freeze.

Her bag slides down past her knee, almost out of reach. "Damn it," she says. She grips me to her chest and at the same time shifts to catch the handle of her purse. *Oops.* I've thrown her off.

She's gritting her teeth as she says, "Don't you know I have a roast in the oven? I've got three kids to pick up after this! Baseball, pimple doctor, fat doctor! All I do is run you kids around."

"But why do we have to come *here*?"

I pull away and wait for the blast: *Whaddya mean why do we have to come? What do-ya think?* But she doesn't say that. Instead she levels that handbag and never drops me. She looks into my eyes and, with a calmness foreign to my mother, says, "I honestly don't know, Eileen. We're here because it's the next step. I have no idea where it's leading but we're going to take it."

I have no idea what this means. Who is this woman? Her brown velvet eyes are on the brink of tears. She is pleading now. I touch the smooth olive skin on her cheek and put my own cheek to hers. It's warm and moist and it feels like we have melted into one. She smells of perfume, cigarettes, and coffee. I'm hooked.

And then she's back to digging into her purse. She finds a nickel and shoves it into the meter. "Got it," she says with pride. I nestle into that place below her chin and against her neck, resigned.

After that we face the plate glass window with its wooden leg dangling like a side of beef over a butcher's counter. Mom's shoulders fall into a slump as she lugs me up to the door. It's a brand new leg hanging there, a man's leg, but it looks antique. It's shameful, really.

**This is a boy everyone loves, I'm sure of it. I figure that if I were the March of Dimes girl people would love me just as much.**

With her arms full, Mom has to headbutt the door to get inside. The waiting room is a hodge-podge of vinyl chairs with thin, oily cushions. Old magazines spill from an end table. There are prayers on the wall. I can't read them but I know they're prayers because they have symbols like fish and folded hands with glowing auras. The place smells of talcum powder, sawdust, and burning metal. Industrial-strength machinery hammers through walls from the backroom, drills and circular saws. There is one other person waiting here, a man as old as my grandpa. He has one empty pant leg, and I'm wondering how he lost that leg. Probably a war, but I don't know that kind of history yet. I try not to stare but his eyes are leveled right at me from behind wire-rimmed glasses. He looks like someone who has just been socked in the jaw. When our eyes meet, his eyes soften from a wince to a misty-eyed, pity-filled look. I curl up in my chair so I'll disappear. *He pities me?*

Most of the prosthetists here are missing a leg, usually from a war. They are the only *amputees* we know. (No one in my family ever calls me an "amputee" except Annie and the sister who is between us in age, Molly. They joke about a make-believe amputee camp they call "Wa-heel-la." They croon the camp's anthem: *Sing around the campfire; throw your wooden leg in! Sing wa-heel-la. Sing wa-heel-la. Work. Whittle. Squiddle!* Our parents cannot fight the grin on this one, so they laugh out loud, and then say, "Stop it! That's so awful!" Even I have to laugh at the cleverness of this song.) Now, a prosthetist staggers past Mom and me. He's toting someone else's leg on his way from the workshop to a fitting room. I get a chill and then goosebumps.

We wait here in the lobby, Mom clutching her giant purse to her lap like a shield.

She checks her panty hose—no runs, thank God. She hates runs. She wears dusty rose lipstick to go with her brown velvet eyes. At times like these, when I have her all to myself, I want to know her as a best friend. I want to forget who we are and why we're sitting here. I want to go to another time and place. I impose myself in her childhood.

When I play this game, Mom is happy to play along. So I say, "I saw you and Mio at the Pogue's Arcade yesterday," and she knows I'm talking about the fourteen-year olds, Joy, and her best friend, Mio. She's not a bit spooked. "What were we doing?"

"You each had a dish of ice cream at the counter in the coffee shop."

Mom arches her back—good posture ranking among her highest values—and smiles. "That sounds about right."

"You had vanilla. And it only cost a nickel." I know this from all of our talks about the Depression.

"A nickel was a lot back then," says Mom. "Graeter's was better, though. It used to be so rich it stuck to the roof of your mouth. For a dime you could suck on a scoop of Graeter's all afternoon."

No kiddin', I think, and I try to imagine it. Then my mouth starts to water. I taste Graeter's mint chip ice cream on the roof of my mouth.

My head drops to my dress. Molly is two years older than me, and I'm wearing her navy blue dress with a white sailor collar. I couldn't wait for her to outgrow it. Now I've gotten grass stains on the collar from rolling downhill on our front lawn. I look back at the old man and his empty pant leg. *Why are we here? What did I do to deserve this?*

Meanwhile, Mom covers her nose to avoid inhaling sawdust—dust, fat, and loose hair being three things that Mom cannot abide—and notes my somber mood. "Ah heck!" This is what she says when she would really like to say something like: "We are so screwed."

I know that I don't belong with these wounded men. I can see that in her eyes.

They call us back to a new fitting room, and it's the same as the last: fiber-wood paneling and a full-length mirror at the end of parallel bars that look to be about a mile long, though they are more like ten feet. We sit in chairs at the head of the bars.

"They're going to put you in your legs today," says Mom, "and you're going to walk between those bars right up to the mirror."

*Really?*

The leg man enters, clutching a wooden leg in each hand. To my nearly five-year-old eyes they look huge and heavy, but they are probably small enough to fit on a large marionette. In fact, they look like marionette legs, except that the below-knee leg—the "BK" as he calls it—has a leather corset to fix onto my thigh, which is attached by metal hinges. Those hinges will bend with my knee. But will they take a chunk of my flesh along the way? The whole contraption seems barbaric. The above-knee leg is shiny wood from the top of the thigh to the tip of its elfin foot.

Standing before me now, the leg man cups the legs in his hands the way Pete Rose grips his baseball bat after he swipes it between his thighs. I'm amazed at the ease with which he handles them. I can't imagine how I will lift them, let alone make them walk.

In his own prosthesis he kneels inside the parallel bars, right in front of my left leg, to attach the BK to my real body. His hands coated in dried goop from somebody else's thigh, he lifts a lamb's-wool sock from the pouch on his rubber apron, shakes it in my face as if he's holding a fancy doll, and asks, "Like that?"

I shrug. Then I remember to smile.

He slides it onto my real leg, covering that part just below my knee. "How's it feel?"

"Good," I say, and strangely enough, it isn't so bad.

I look down at his part: a chalky white line against slicked black hair flecked with sawdust and talcum. This man seems more suited to roll under a car and poke around like the mechanics in Dad's car dealership than to wrap his hands around my thigh.

But this is my future: I will look onto the crowns of others as they kneel before me, my princes, who do not bring glass slippers for my feet.

Mom is now twisted like a cinnamon roll in her chair, eyes wide, not saying a word. The ash on her cigarette is again dangerously long.

The leg man slides the artificial leg over my sock. I'm stuffed inside. He laces the corset around my thigh, pulling tight so it won't come off. My leg goes numb. I see my face in the mirror: brows knitted, colorless lips pressed tight. Mom is next to me, a haze of cigarette smoke her halo, she's stunned. I want to tell the leg man about the tightness but he already notes my distress. "You'll get used to that," he says.

*Huh?*

"Stand up."

*Stand?* Stand on a baseball bat with metal jaws? I feel stupid for asking but I say, "How?"

"Well," says Mom, flatly, before she escalates to a shriek, "Just like anyone else!" She's thrusting her arms out, her body language scolding me: *Isn't it obvious?* Her cigarette is now a filter with two inches of ash. A chunk breaks off, landing on a floor that has seen worse, I'm sure of it.

I look at her in the mirror; she's crossed her legs but she's still holding her arms out. "Come on!" she bellows. With her arms held out like a saint before execution, I'm just certain that she is playing her whole afternoon out in her head: *baseball, pimple doctor, fat doctor, roast! And get that Eileen into a pair of legs, damn it!*

And to this I'm thinking: *Over. My. Dead. Body!* I push back into my seat and cross my arms.

She comes forward to get right in my face. "Whaddya think you're doin'?" she whispers. There is silky black down on Mom's olive skin. It's so fine that to me, with my fairer complexion, basset-hound eyes, and hair a mixture of elements: copper, gold and Midwestern mud, I view Mom's silky black down as a mark of pedigree, a symbol of what I have yet to achieve. That is, if I ever grow into it. But now with her eyes bulging and her jaw quivering under the down, I imagine she's sprouting a beard. My mouth goes sour; my eyes fill with tears. Who is this woman?

She freezes.

Now, with her fists at her sides, she snarls, "Oooh, I-lean!" and slams back into her seat, where she tosses her head back. "What am I gonna do with you?" She raises a fist to the ceiling and puffs at bangs that are not falling. With her jaw jutting out like this she stresses every syllable, and adds a few of her own. "Will-la I e-verrrr win with this chi-old?"

Then she starts to cry.

I slump low in my seat, my bangs hiding my face so I can peer at her without her seeing my tears. And the leg man is soothing her. "Ah, now, come on. You'll be fine."

I've done it again. I've brought out The Nervous Wreck. Some people slow down when they get anxious; Mom pushes harder.

I rub my index finger over one of the shiny metal pinchers on my new leg. They are every bit as sharp as they look. *Get me out of here!* I want to bang my head against the wall. Instead, I grab one of those parallel bars and yank myself up. The metal pinchers begin to clamp shut as my knee straightens toward a standing position. I'm just praying that there is no fat in their path.

The leg man shouts, "There you go! That's it."

I squeeze every muscle and break out in sweat. I tug and pull and when I'm finally standing, I see a girl staring back at me in the mirror. The sweat chills when I realize it's me. I sway forward, then back. I tighten my grip on the bar and stretch to grab hold of the other bar but that throws everything out of balance.

My right side, with no leg to anchor it, pitches forward. "Grab her!" yells Mom.

She tosses her cigarette butt and jumps up, but she grabs her handbag instead and clutches it in front of her like someone watching a car swerve to miss her before slamming into a brick wall. Meanwhile, on his knees, the leg man throws a hand to my belly like Johnny Bench's baseball glove goes up on a strike out pitch. He catches me.

And I'm steady, although I still can't reach the other bar.

"Could you help her stand?" he asks Mom, impatiently.

She lunges to prop me up by digging her fingernails into my armpits; her purse jammed into my back somehow levels me. "See that? You're doing it," she says to the mirror.

*No, you are*, I say back to her image in my head.

"Now," he says, "guide her hand to the other bar. Good. She has to get used to standing alone. Okay. Let go."

"Are you crazy?" says Mom's eyebrows in the mirror.

My eyes sweep down the mirror from her face to myself standing beneath her. I still can't believe it's me and yet it's the way I've always imagined myself. I'm a whole girl. And, even better, I will no longer have to squiddle. I will be one who walks.

I smile at myself in the mirror until I notice the flesh toppling over this corset like a doughnut. No wonder it hurts. I'm not a fat kid, not even chubby, but every ounce of baby fat on that thigh is being wrenched by this corset like hands squeezing a throat.

I don't want to look, but I can't tear my eyes away from it.

The muscles inside of my thigh tighten and cramp. This is too hard, and I'm even holding the bars. How will I walk outside on the street? And then I think: *Once a squiddler, always a squiddler.* My knee wobbles.

The leg man grimaces. "Sit down. I don't like how it's fitting."

*He* doesn't like how it's fitting? I fall onto my seat, relieved, jubilant, and now that I'm invested: a Nervous Wreck.

The leg man has already disappeared. He's taken both legs back to his workshop. I haven't even tried on the second. In the mirror I zero in on the grass stains. My ecstasy deflates with every clang from the workroom machinery. There is buzzing, hammering, and a noise unlike anything in the civilized world, a noise so shrill it hurts my teeth and lingers. It takes me out of my body, while my head fills with more questions: What if these legs don't work? Can I do this? Why do I have to do this? What sin have I committed?

I ask my mother The Question again. It's the same one I've been asking since I first realized that I'm different. Mom is so sick of The Question. We get it from the faces of strangers every time she takes me out of the neighborhood. Though few people actually say it, their body language is uniform: first, there is the generous smile one offers to a small child; then, the troubled look as the eyes meet the hem of my skirt and find nothing else; next the eyes widen as the jaw atrophies; finally, what's left is The Question plastered over that O-shaped mouth, *What happened to that child?!* This is what their expressions scream at us *before* they turn away.

Now, sitting here in The Hanger with my hopes pinned to a life of hauling my weight on wood and leather corsets with metal pinchers versus a life of squiddling, I realize something about my life, something which no five-year-old words could describe, something like *I am so screwed!*

And with all of this anger pitted against my guilt over disappointing Mom, I cannot hold my tongue another second. I must ask: "Mom, why was I born without legs?"

But she has her answer ready. She can now *feel* when The Question is coming, and although she swallows like she's nauseous, she manages to barely raise a brow as she says in what is, for my mother, a strangely even tone, "When you were born, Dr. G. handed you to me and said, 'Joy, your baby doesn't have any legs.' But I hugged you and said, 'Eileen is my four-leaf clover'."

This doesn't answer my question. Still, I'm momentarily lured away from it because I so want to believe her story. I want to be the most hoped for baby, the grand prize of children. The four-leaf clover!

But does she really want a four-leaf clover, this same woman who once drew pen-and-ink models like the newspaper ads, models with long legs and high heels?

Now, as Mom and I sit in the leg man's fitting room, saws and drills grinding so that I am transcended to other places and times, I am still innocent of this truth, or story, whatever this narrative about my birth will be, and of why it has to become mine. I'm looking into my mother's eyes and thinking: *A four-leaf clover is nice enough, but couldn't I have legs instead?*

Mom reads my face and sighs dolefully. "Oh, Eileen. If I could give you mine I would." And for a moment I believe she would do that. I wonder how doctors do that, put one set of legs on another body? I'm giddy at the prospect. Until I realize that my brothers and sisters would never go for it. *Take Mom's legs?*

I shake my head. The very thought incites a riot inside of me. I'm twisting in my oily, vinyl seat, knotted up in a ball of rage. "Now, that's enough!" she whispers. Then she digs through her purse for another cigarette. I stand on my chair and demand an answer. "Why?! But *why* was I born without legs? What happened to me?"

I stop just shy of saying what I really want to say, which is, "Why *me*?" Still, I've gone too far. She can tell that I wish it were someone else by my tone. I see her bottom lip tuck itself into her mouth like a problem solved. The roots of my hair prickle my scalp from goose bumps. I'm a tattle tale; I want to put *all* the blame on someone else. And that to Mom is an atrocity, shirking responsibility, the lowest of crimes.

She has stopped scrambling, and now she drops her purse. I steady myself for the backlash by gripping the torn arms of this cold chair. I know the answer before she speaks. My mouth turns dry as chalk as my eyes fill with tears.

In the full-length mirror I see myself in Molly's old dress, the collar stained, and Mom, who is wearing the sure smile of a Bible salesman. My stomach twists and tightens so that I might stop breathing, except that my heart is pounding too hard.

"You don't have legs," says Mom with a tap on my nose. "You don't have legs because baby Jesus chose *you* to carry the cross!"

My face in the mirror goes pale, so pale that I might disappear. I don't want to carry a cross. I don't like what it says about me. It's not an honor; it's a penance. Tears rush in and I'm blinded by them. I just have to keep hold of that image, the one of myself standing up, but bitter tears are now in the way. I fight to hold onto that whole girl. I know that's who I am, and who I'm supposed to be. When I see how others look at me, I lose sight of her. She must be there. She could be staring back at me right now.


Years after I've learned to walk, and after which I have *not* been contacted by the March of Dimes, I will find myself back here for a teenager's pair of legs. By then, Mom will have become so burned out on The Hanger that she simply will not do it anymore. Then she will pull up to the door, gunning the engine as if ready to jump the curb and crash through the plate glass, before slamming on the brakes. With the leg dangling above us in the window, she'll say, "Molly will pick you up when she gets out of school."

Later, in a waiting room full of Vietnam Vets, I'll stare at the plaque with the Serenity Prayer on it. There, among some of the most wounded men in American history, I will sit, my own ego sawed in half, and I'll try to make sense of that damn prayer. To me, the whole thing will boil down to this: "God, give me the *code* (not the wisdom, not the courage, and what the hell use is serenity, anyway?) Just give me the *damn code* for how to 'change' all of this."

# Peter E. Murphy
# Aspirin

I swallowed a handful after a pitcher
of beer did not get me high enough. Maybe
that's why I fell, swinging at a softball,
into a manhole in Central Park.
The pitch was sweet as I stepped into it.
The metal lid we called home was wobbly
after a player who climbed down, climbed back
up relieved, having taken a piss.
Because I wanted to be somebody
I tried things I knew I couldn't do.
I swung. I missed. I fell into a hole.
Gravity pulled me like a planet, a plant.
I take a low dose each night to thin my blood.
My clogged heart troubles me; it's still aspiring.

# Federal Reserve

WHAT'S THE USE OF HAPPINESS IF IT CAN'T BUY YOU MONEY? —HENNY YOUNGMAN

When you leave the free tour of "Money in Motion"
they hand you a cellophane sack of shredded bills good
for nothing. But you can take it home to your kid,

if you have one, or just forget about it, which I did,
until finding it in my pocket as I step on a bus
without a token or change that is exact.

The driver apologizes, but does not offer a free ride.
So I back off and walk to work, bleary-eyed and late,
thinking of history and money—too much of one,

not enough of the other. How currency divided the colonies
when they turned uncivil. How as the war progressed, the size
of Southern notes inflated until growing worthless.

Lincoln looks old and ill on the new $5 bill which claims
to be *Safer, Smarter and More Secure*. His cheeks
are sallow and his face is tinged in purple dye.

At the counterfeit exhibit I fail to detect the phonies.
Like most of my bad choices, they all look good to me,
except in hindsight wondering how could I be so blind?

They shred millions of bills a day, mostly singles,
like myself. I've shed a wife who kept my son, two dogs,
a girlfriend who went bad and started to bite.

My own bills are based on take-out and television.
When the Berlin Wall fell I saw graffiti on the news—
*We came, we saw, we did a little shopping.*

I never put value in stocks, although I wouldn't refuse
an option. But unlike the colony of New Hampshire,
issuing both Continental *and* Spanish dollars,

I would like to live free and *not* die.

# To Kill an Albatross

FROM *THE MAN WHO NEVER WAS*


WHEN A MAN TELLS YOU THAT HE GOT RICH THROUGH HARD WORK, ASK HIM WHOSE?


The man who never was
lumbers up the stairs to the condominiums
where he will do maximum work
for minimum wage.

If he had a name it might be Peter Murphy
converting punk to dust.
It might be Garry Morgan tramping
through Wales looking for his head.

He mops himself
into an electrical room where the doors are alarmed
and the buttons depressed.
He is afraid of embellished charges, of adult emissions.

He is afraid of occupational language,
of press releases and masking tape.
He is afraid he will deplete his dialogue bank—
When all his words are exhausted he will die.

Around his neck hangs the figure
of a smaller man chained to a piece of wood.
If this man had a name it might be Jesus Christ.
It might be Albert Ross.

The man who never was dreams his body
commutes from home to office bearing a tie and a jacket,
a brief case of important papers. And in the suburbs,
a wife, a child or two, a dog that does not bite.

# Eamon Grennan
# Collage with Helicopter, Cottage, Drowned Man

On the one hand your neighbor puts finishing touches to the interior of the cottage
his father lived and died in, that surrendered at last to the clasp of weeds and grass
and sycamore leaves, to all small things that embrace and multiply in the slow ooze of
decay as if not flesh but consciousness itself, its continuity, were in question. But now
the house has been brought back to dryness, its blind gaps translated to the glazed
gaze of windows beaming behind hedges, its fresh slates gleaming their glad sense
of *containment*. And now the man stands under his electrician's light surveying his
handiwork, wiping his face clean of dust with a crumpled hanky. On the other hand,
you know the sound chopping out of heavy cloud is the navy helicopter searching for
the hotel piano-player who's gone missing between this near shore and the island he,
a strong swimmer, was heading for, and whose fingers are tangled now in knots of
kelp, his good ears gone deaf to everything, even the drone of the coming and going
of the sea that spills in and out of them as if they were shells, fine spiraling shells
from which all breathing sea-life has migrated. Always this two-handed reel of the
real, a sort of innocent indifferent wind that *mouths its constant smatter throughout
space*—to leave us speechless, at a loss to say what's behind it. And now, sitting outside, circled by fallen leaves and birdsong, you catch the hum of autumn bees that
with no buzzing fuss gather and gather but give you no name for what goes on here
as the year rolls towards its terminus, neither the flush of fruit coming into its own
nor the fretted edges the first frost will startle the grass with, only the rustle of leaves
round your feet, a slow scratch-sound that seems to speak a truth almost abstract,
although in fact it's all fact, caught fast in the ceaseless flow of things, athwart which

comes the sudden crack again of the helicopter's *hacka-hacka* and you have to sense again how the underwater thrum of waves is ghosted by jellyfish and slow weed, have to know the missing swimmer is homing now among wreaths of bladderwrack, is floating under the lorn, lone sign of the curlew—the bird's high cry keening him.

# Conflagration Revisited

CE MONDE N'EST QUE LA CRETE D'UN INVISIBLE INCENDIE. —JACCOTTET, *AIRS*

Trees winter-stripped to a few gold leftovers
clinging to willows; the oak a scuffed chestful
of dry browns rattling at every breeze:
what he remembers is something like a book
learned page by page by heart
as if nothing else mattered: eyes in flight
flung headlong into every hard fact
until all was conflagration, the tip of things
a world of hot tongues whispering *grace-this, grace-that*
as if it meant something, meant he'd come upon
a destination unplanned but recognized
as what he'd been after—a place where
after the ignition of bodies
there was no remainder, where even soul
seemed possible, was not just smoke.

# Going Back

WHAT WOULD IT BE TO BE WATER, ONE BODY OF WATER . . .

—MARIE PONSOT, "SPRINGING"

What if a going back to water
were the chosen way?
To immerse: let limb by limb,
appendage, member, drift
to fluency, a permeable
positive transparency:
to lose all alphabets
and other perturbations
for the pure lap and slither,
the very *oh* sloth of
simple drift, be nothing
but a boneless, see-through,
barely swimming unicell
before anything, all agog
and afloat in a wordless
soup of sensory (sort of)
cognitives, dead set
on the staying power
of the mere glitter
of being itself, perdurable
and simple, till live liquid
gives up even the last ghost

of the ghost of a last chance
of becoming anything
but a bubble of light
with all the action
of the wide world captured
in its spectral glimmer-sphere
of rainbows, its constellation
of radiant ache, a truly new
beyond-all-known-elements
unspoken universe
holding an almost readable sign
haloed over what
you'd take for an entryway,
seeing words
in one of the tongues
you've cut yourself off from—
spelling out *it's white, white . . .*
*a heart-jet, a river,*
so you start over again
as if you'd never felt
at home on earth's
solidity, nor even there

*where a new succession*
*sings and flies—*
beyond question
or appetite
or expectation.

# Splitting Instant

When a sudden skin-drenching rain-squall
suddenly stopped and wet light oozed
through cloud and everything grew jeweled,
as if Hopkins had taken his word
to the weather—saying *Diamantine!*
so mud in the drained lake
received a metal sheen and gleamed
like the mud of Paradise might have gleamed—
was when the sawtooth cry of the redtail hawk
brought me to a stop, seeing small birds flee
as the big broadwing floated over,
splitting the still sleek air with the sound
—jagged, metallic—of his hunger. Such moments:
nothing to be done or said, seeing
the blood-berries of the holly bush
burning their lace of Christmas illuminations
under rain that's beginning again, the cloud
that split to let sunshine through
having—even in the ticking instant I stopped
to look up, let my skin sense it—closed over.

# Lawrence-Minh Bùi Davis
# Like Kissing Your Sister

In the spring of 1977 my uncle was stranded at sea for forty-nine days. He narrowly avoided capture by South Sea pirates, then shipwrecked on a deserted island near Malaysia. Sun-stroked and delirious, he dreamed of the days before he escaped Vietnam, when he was held in a prison camp and tortured promptly every Friday.

My cousin, his youngest son, now attends private school.

My cousin's name is Vuong, but he goes by Henri. He's seventeen. He and his family live in a lavishly restored eighteenth-century hotel in Lausanne, Switzerland. Henri dresses like a Swiss boy, which is to say, from an American perspective, way too Euro: neat, tight, rich, effeminate.

I grew up a few thousand miles away in Falls Church, Virginia. My father has an emigration story roughly similar to my uncle's, but he's never told it. Facing the prospect of further imprisonment in the reeducation camps, he too escaped Vietnam sometime in the late 1970s. But that's all he'll say.

According to Henri, his father lost his soul on the exodus from Vietnam. I'm inclined to think the same of my father, only for "soul" I'd substitute "sense of humor."

The Swiss by and large are carefully dressed, tall, and trim. Circa 2008 Uncle Thanh is carefully dressed, average height, and fat. It's hard to imagine him as he must have been on that island—emaciated, not far from death, scratching out poetry in place of eating. Now an über-wealthy Swiss banker, he can afford what all Vietnamese of his vintage once dreamed of: an endless procession of European food. His delectations of choice: palmiers, profiteroles, and thin, pale yellow French mayonnaise, slathered on skinny baguettes that stretch to an ever-extending horizon (his words exactly).

Asian women are not attractive.

Says Henri. There are no other Vietnamese in Lausanne, not one, no Asians of any stripe besides tourists, so my cousin equates feminine Asian features with his sisters. To Henri only Euros are attractive; kissing an Asian would be equivalent to kissing one of his sisters.

A literal equivalence, that is. To his knowledge there is no Swiss (or French, or German, or Vietnamese) saying for "that's like kissing your sister," as in, "earning second place is like kissing your sister." It's just one of those things that doesn't translate very well. Not too easy explaining the American English meaning to him—*no, no, we're not really talking about incest, Henri*—but once he catches on, he's fascinated.

Young Henri fancies himself a poet, and a language connoisseur, like his father before him. He hopes to become the first Viet-Swiss poet of prominence. There are Swiss-Viet poets living in Vietnam, writing in Vietnamese, he explains, but no Viet-Swiss living in Switzerland, writing in French and English and German, blah blah blah blah blah, I always tune him out at this point. All his conjecture seems pointless to me, as his poetry is crap. He's not going to be the first anything. But I have to admire his insistence on greatness in the face of incompetence: it's his most American quality.

Also, paradoxically, his most Vietnamese.

These days poetry has little purchase with young people in the U.S., but it's strangely popular on the campus of my college, the not-very-esteemed College of Northeastern Virginia. For the last two years CNV students have been treated to the literary stylings of an anonymous "campus bard," who scrawls his chalk verses on the sidewalk outside the Student Center.

The concluding lines of his most famous poem:

2 rides diverged @ the kegger
and i chose the sorority girl
less banged

For days after the poem appeared, students prevented campus groundskeepers from washing it away. The photography club was eventually enlisted to preserve it permanently. Conventional wisdom says the final lines should be read figuratively, as there isn't, at least not at CNV, such a thing as a "less banged sorority girl." That's like saying a "less tall redwood." So the *choice less banged*, according to popular interpretations, must be a non-choice, a turning away from choosing entirely—either failure to pick a major, failure to graduate, or suicide. All three are fairly common at CNV.

At the end of next year, Uncle Thanh plans to make a return trip. Not to Vietnam, but his deserted island. His therapist can't decide whether or not she supports the venture, but I don't think my uncle will be denied no matter what she says; he's been plotting latitude-longitude

# 2 rides diverged @ the kegger and i chose the sorority girl less banged

figures for some time now, estimating precisely where he spent the lonely year of 1977. Henri wants to accompany him and write a book of poems about the experience. A father-son adventure for the twenty-first century: simulated, not-harrowing, looks pretty good on the college application.

But maybe it will be harrowing, says my father quietly. To return is to relive the trauma, the Robinson Crusoe isolation, the physical deprivation. The fever-dream of exile—as soon as he managed to escape Vietnam, my uncle longed to get back in. And the pirates, looming at the edge of the horizon—that black fleck, the foul wind, specter of salt on the tongue . . . I sometimes get the impression my uncle *was* captured and simply doesn't admit it. He's changed the story, even in his own memory.

I know my father has changed his—he's erased it entirely.

Maybe erasure is the theme of the larger, collective story. We know now there were as many as three million boat people; of that number, several hundred thousand, maybe as many 750,000, perished at sea, erased forever from human history.

But as Henri puts it, and rather well for him, I think,

we breed like rabbits,
like flies,
like bad moods.

The Viet Diaspora staggers on.

The Cluck-U Chicken franchise was founded in New Brunswick, New Jersey, in 1985 by enterprising then–Rutgers University sophomore Robert Ilvento. Since then Cluck-U has expanded to include hundreds of locations in over fifteen states, and hopes by 2010 to place a restaurant near every college campus in America. Cluck-U's specialty, and most popular product: hot wings.

On the CNV campus, particularly with the fraternity set, Cluck-U wings are the late-night food du jour, the hotter the better. The choices range from mild to atomic to nuclear to thermo-nuclear, with each one progressively hotter.

Not on the everyday menu: the legendary 911 wings. To purchase them one must sign a legal waiver. Successful completion of a full order of twelve wings earns one a free tee shirt and a place of honor on the wall. Unsurprisingly a considerable mythology has developed; CNV's Cluck-U has two pictures up, and many claim to know or know of the honorees.

**Ideally one should sweat profusely while eating. Suffering equals comfort equals cultural currency.**

That guy did it but had to have emergency surgery a few days later.

This one had his stomach replaced as a kid, has an artificial stomach made of reinforced plastic—that's how he could handle the 911 wings.

Heard of another guy, from another state, who ate fifteen.

Special unit in a lot of ERs for 911 wings patients.

Knew someone who tried and failed, ended up dead.

Another popular story: Cluck-U factories close on the day the sauce for the 911 wings is made. Clear out all the workers to avoid a potential lawsuit—the sauce is that hot, the fumes toxic. Three guys in hazard suits stir with twenty–foot poles.

Another story, supposedly confirmed by a real live Cluck-U employee: a major ingredient in the sauce is law enforcement-grade mace. Normally utilized, of course, for pacifying unruly mobs. Thus Cluck-U quietly refigures and valorizes State control. It effectively replaces the unpalatable image of a policeman spraying lethal mist into a crowd with the innocuous picture of an eager young person, consuming extra-spicy chicken wings in a heroic effort. The Heel of the State is not forced upon the populace but eagerly and reverently embraced.

This is the graduate student reading, and we all know graduate students have the time to think up this kind of nonsense when everyone else is busy having sex.

The truer campus consensus is this: 911 wings are the height of ___. Fill in the blank with the desired category: masculinity, heroism, sexual potency, and so on.

I can understand this mentality. The ability to withstand spicy food is a moronic point of pride for Viets around the globe. In the MD/DC/VA corridor of the

Viet Diaspora, the comfort food of choice is gà xào sả ớt, or chicken stir-fried with lemongrass and chilies. The more ớt, the better the gà xào sả ớt. Ideally one should sweat profusely while eating. Suffering equals comfort equals cultural currency.

Despite his flamboyant Swiss-ness, Henri has me beat by a wide margin when it comes to heat-tolerance. I've cultivated mine for a long time—a disciplined regimen of Thai bird chilies and Scotch Bonnets, sometimes habañeros—so this discovery was quite damaging to my pride. To give you an idea of what's invested here: for years one of our cousins has roamed the LA bar-scene, challenging all male patrons to shots of the worst hot-sauce on hand, first to drink water loses. Should her opponent drink first, he covers her tab for the night; should she drink first, she goes home and fucks him.

In her wake is a long string of bleary-eyed, retching Los Angelinos. Mostly Hollywood-studio types, apparently. In my family we speak of her exploits with extreme reverence.

Henri and his family come to visit the U.S. during CNV's spring semester of 2005. Ostensibly Henri wants to add a new "dimension" to his poetics, or some such nonsense. Go inside the "War Machine." He's also considering applying to some American universities. I think part of him buys into the widespread European propaganda that American girls are easy, which, to be fair, a visit to an American university probably won't disprove.

I'll skip over his cursory introduction to American culture, with the expected episodes of awkwardness and amusement. Knowing full well his extraordinary capacity for heat, I see our destination clearly before he ever even arrives: Cluck-U and the 911 wings. I will prove myself vicariously through my cousin, with his white Capri pants and fondness for bouncy Swiss techno music.

The day of, we decide to bring along my girlfriend Thi, who, as it turns out, can also stand hotter foods than I can. But she grew up in Vietnam, I like to tell myself. Henri stares at her legs unabashedly. I take pictures of everything for documentary purposes. I'll show them at the frat house and the next VSA (Viet Student Assoc.) meeting.

We're inside. We order. The cashier doesn't bat an eyelid, nor, it seems, does the sleepy young man who prepares them (wearing heavy latex gloves). We carry the 911 wings from the counter to our table without much fanfare. Henri's hair is styled annoyingly, I notice just now, spiky in the front, faux-mullet in the back. I briefly explain to him the significance of eating the wings, as well as their reputed level of heat.

*Do not to worry*, he insists. *This is what you eat when you are watching the pro football, no? To me they are not to be spicy.*

The sauce's consistency is nearly like toothpaste. Instead of the usual liquid-red color, it's matte orange. The air above the wings is hazy, like truck exhaust, and even from a distance of two to three feet, the fumes make my eyes tear up. I have already determined I won't be trying any wings; instead I dip my pinky into the sauce for a microdot-sized taste.

To preserve my pride, I will quickly gloss over my inadequacy and move on to Henri's attempt.

Henri eats two, three wings. They are hot in his mouth, but not too hot, he says. He eats another few wings. He licks the sauce from his fingers somewhat like a rooster might prance across a barnyard.

Then he stops. I take a picture, though I sense what must be coming. Or maybe *because* I sense it. The heat is registering in his stomach just now. His face, one that has never needed a shave, is suddenly beading with sweat.

"I dee-ew nut feel tew guhd," he says. This mock-phonetic reproduction is a slight exaggeration, yes, but some sense of his accent is necessary, precisely at this moment, which is why I've waited to unveil it.

Minutes later he is throwing up in a trashcan in the parking lot. Thi goes into Safeway, buys him yogurt, a single-serving-size carton of whole milk, and a bottle of Pepto-Bismol, and he's eventually fine. But that's getting away from the moment, when anything could have happened. The sauce could have burned through his stomach lining. He could have had an allergic reaction, seizures. Shock. Heart attack. Or heroism, that too was still feasible—back to finish the rest of the wings. Tee shirt and a picture on the wall. A spectrum of possibility.

One cannot help but think back thirty years, all the way across the Pacific, to my uncle on his island, retching in the beach-sand. He suffers from sun poisoning, vitamin deficiency, dehydration, fear, despair. There's no sense of a rich future. He may very well die on the island, never start a new life. Have children, grandchildren. Pass along his carefully preserved poetry, the collected, smuggled works of a dozen censored Viet poets. All fade away.

Night is coming. Vertigo and the half-madness of starvation. And the pirates are drawing nearer, red-rimmed eyes shining, cocks swelling, fingers itching. Their ships moving faster now.

The bile blistering up Henri's throat . . .

"& so we beat off/," writes the campus bard, on the sidewalk outside the CNV Student Center, "boats against the current."

# Jim Daniels
# Sweating It Out

She lives with another guy.
He's going to be pissed.

Fan waves futile against
Morning's thick muffle, stuttering

above the clock's quiet grind.
She wants a cigarette

and to go home, get it over
with. Just a night in a bar

that got out of hand. Their bodies
map sweat onto pale sheets.

*What did you expect*—she grabs
his erection—*when you steer*

*with this?* A fertilized field blows
stink in the open window. *How*

*do you live with that?* she asks.
*You have a great body,* he says

to say something true. *You like it,*
*huh?* They turn from each other

to dress. He drives her home.
She slams the door.

Back home, he dowses hot sauce
on eggs. His shirt soaked. Sweat,

he can't get enough, poison oozing out
into the daily stink

while the interesting story goes on
miles away.

# Losing the License

Sixteen, I stayed home to work my first job while my parents

went camping. Jean was her name. Jean Suguro. She was

and is a year older than me. Smart enough to be unhappy

in our factory suburb where her brilliant father made equations

into cars and her mother lived quietly sad in their dark, shuttered house.

My father counted car parts at the other end. Jean had a boyfriend

at the other end. Handsome David who turned out to be gay.

While my parents were toasting marshmallows at Burt Lake—

my little brother, sitting too close, melted his sneakers—

Jean arrived in her Beetle. She'd sit on my lap in the front seat

and ride me in the half-shade of streetlights through thick leaves.

But that night, we had a bed. Her long black hair covered

and uncovered her breasts, a dark wave rolling in and out.

She slipped off a short jean skirt. Her almond skin glistened

in my black-lit room above and below her glowing white panties.

I kicked off my jeans. We rolled together on electric sheets,

our bodies crackling sparks. We showered, then went at it again till dawn.

In the morning, on hands and knees, I gathered long black hair from the white tub.

I was helpless against her, David be damned.

My license was missing. I drove to the station for another.

Later, I found the first—lodged between mattress and box spring.

Jean gave me lice via David, and since I had lost my license and now had two, my anger burned outrageously. Sixteen twice.

For days I circled her quiet house with tainted wonder and explosive ache

till I lurched to a stop and spilled onto her yard wailing in agony.

She emerged and took me back into her arms while her mother shouted Japanese.

My shoes melted.

# Sinking the Cigarette Boat, Miami

I drove it into the middle of the bay
the deep snarl rumble mocking discretion—
I cut the engine. No time to stray or stay.
A friend trailing in a row boat. Contempt
scoured me. Or fear. Or paranoia. Or just
whatever drugs were thumping through
my veins. Two guys I'd trusted got busted,
and cops were sniffing my dollar bills. I knew

the more I destroyed, the less was true.
No time to pray or pay. Ten years washed ashore
like coke residue, tiny grains I could barely
imagine. The habit was wanting more.
I leapt into the little boat, then blew a hole in mine.
It didn't take much aim. Like doing a line.

# Norman Simon
# ESPN

In the stars live beings of fire. Their greatest pleasure is to merge—body on body, flame into flame. Maggie is fire. She became that in the crematorium on Long Island, while I was left behind. But I dream that I am fire, too. Soon, I'll join her.

"Mr. Perelman, where are you? It's lunchtime."

"I'm here."

"You think you could sit up for me?"

She helps me. Over on my hip, then push with my legs, like doing the side-stroke. Swimming across Lake Peekskill, my father trailing me in the rowboat, just in case. Strong, I felt strong.

"Come on, Mr. Perelman. Don't quit on me now."

I push, she pulls. She props the pillow behind me, tray on my lap. I can smell mashed potatoes, I can see red Jell-O.

"You want to feed yourself today?"

I look. Who is it? Yelena? No, not her; she's got a Russian accent like my grand-mother. Maybe it's Gypsy? No—Gypsy had fat black arms. Used to put me on the toilet. *Do your business, little man.* My aunt Millie? Sounds like her. But how could it be? She's out on Long Island, too.

"Don't feel up to it this afternoon? You should be ashamed of yourself, Mr. Perelman. Making me feed you like a baby."

Jell-O red, potato smell. Who gives a shit?

"If you don't start eating better, we'll have to hook you up to the tube again. You want that?"

Beings of fire, blazing up in the stars. Maggie loved the beach, the sun. No wonder she chose fire. We talked about it before she went. Her hair was gone. Red wig. She laughed. It was easier for her. She was going, I was staying.

"Hey, Mr. Perelman. Somebody here for you."

This one *is* black. Not like Gypsy, though. Where's mama, Gypsy? *She gone. Poor little boy—she gone.*

"Sit up, Mr. Perelman."

"That's okay," someone says.

Maybe it's the television. "Turn that set down, Gypsy."

"Some days he's better than this."

"That's okay. I'll just sit with him."

One time we went to Fire Island. Maggie and me. Took the train to Bayshore, ferry out to Kismet. It was early in the season, a weekday, hardly anyone there. We spread our blanket under the dunes, out of the wind. Too cold to swim. I rubbed her with Coppertone. She always had to watch out for her skin. Redhead, lots of freckles and spots. Lying on her stomach, while I rubbed it in her back and legs. "I told my mother," she said. "I told her your name."

Whoever it was must be gone, or maybe it was just ESPN. Yelena turns it on for me. It's nice of her, but what do I need ESPN for? I used to go to Yankee Stadium with my father, down the stairs at 86$^{th}$ Street, the express coming, I got close to the edge, he let me but holding my hand; the train shaking, the darkness rushing by, 125$^{th}$, 149$^{th}$, holding his hand, then the train coming out of the tunnel and we saw the Stadium, and the hotel, the Concourse Plaza.

I don't sleep too well at night. I dream of fire, inside me and outside. It hurts at night, even though Millie gives me something. No, it couldn't be Millie. She's out in the cemetery on Long Island.

"How are you doing, Mr. Perelman?"

It's ESPN again. I know the voice. I've never been very good with faces, but voices are another thing.

"You feeling all right? Is there anything you need?"

I can turn myself when I want to. Right hip over to left hip, right cheek of my ass to left one, right elbow to left elbow. ESPN has a jaw like Nixon's, but a big guy, big chest, black hair.

"Richard Boyle."

Another Dick.

"They told me your name is Jerry." He holds his hand out. It's cold. Not like Gypsy's hand.

"I'll be coming around to keep you company—a few times a week, or more if you like."

Jerry's dick.

"Maybe we can talk sometimes."

"Nobody calls me Jerry. They call me Salt."

"Were you in the Navy? Merchant Marine?"

I was in nothing. Not even the Boy Scouts. I never liked joining things. Milk and cookies is what I liked. Aunt Millie, one more? *I'm your mother now. Call me Millie, darling, or call me mama.*

"I was in the Navy," ESPN says.

I'm getting tired of talking to him. I wish Yelena would come. Wash me, give me my shot. She had a hard life. No toilet paper in Russia. No eggs. She put newspaper in her boots. Cold winter, long winter, not like here. Shortages. I was called "Salt" because I'd empty the shaker out. Even on French fries, even on eggs and bacon, even in beer. Nobody made me stop until Maggie. Nobody loved me enough before that.

> # I was called "Salt" because I'd empty the shaker out. Even on French fries, even on eggs and bacon, even in beer. Nobody made me stop until Maggie.

I think that ESPN is gone. He must have walked out when I turned my back for a minute. There was a guy in the bed next door. I had to share Millie with him. She pulled the curtains around him and took a lot of time. They don't come to you here if you make a fuss. You have to smile and be charming. Or, if you can't do that, being shy is next best. I'm pretty good at that. I don't want everyone knowing my secrets.

The guy next door is fire now. Fire or dirt. Gypsy found him, and fifteen minutes later they had him out, stripped the bed and had it ready for the next customer. No one was there when he died. No one visited. It doesn't matter. He's fire now. Or maybe dirt. If Maggie had wanted that, I would have followed her, but it wasn't my first choice. My father is dirt, and Millie, and my mother, in Los Angeles or wherever she went. Why would I want to be underground with them?

"Yelena, can I have my shot now?"

"No shot. I explain to you. Doctor say pill. Put in mouth. Drink water."

It hurts, Millie. *Don't be a baby. A spanking, it's nothing.* Then, afterward, pressing me against her. Bad cop, good cop. I swallow the pill. "You want TV on?" I can't understand the television. I used to be able. Now it goes too fast. The people jerk around like a cartoon. Only if it's baseball, I can watch sometimes. Joe DiMaggio and Johnny Lindell and Charlie Keller. My father took me.

"Is there baseball?"

"I don't know baseball."

Maybe I should talk Russian to her. I used to know some words. My grandmother spoke the language. Old lady in a *babushka*. That's one word! *Papirosa. Morozhenoe*. "Don't understand," Yelena says. "English bad." She puts on some channel with the people jerking around. She straightens the covers. Pats my cheek, shaking her head.

Maybe it isn't even baseball season, maybe it's winter.

I open my eyes and ESPN is sitting there. Reading the *New York Times*. I may not be able to understand television anymore, but I can still tell the *New York Times* from the *Daily News*. ESPN has got the paper folded like he's reading it on the subway. "Hey, ESPN—where'd you come from?"

"You're awake, Mr. Perelman. I came from home."

"You live up in the Bronx?"

"No, in Manhattan. Actually, I'm close enough to walk over."

I don't know where I live. Does this place have a name? Ask ESPN—I'll bet he knows. "What's this place called?"

"Beth Jeshurun Center."

I'm in a Jewish place. I don't know why. I'm as Jewish as the next guy, but Maggie wasn't. Her mother wasn't very happy about the whole thing when Maggie let her know. We kept waiting for her to die—not a nice thing to say, but it was true—but she wouldn't. Finally, Maggie had to tell her.

"By the way, Salt, I brought you something. Let me open it up for you."

Cookies. They look like Mallomars, but bigger. "They go good with milk."

"I'll try to get you some," he says.

He comes back with a little half pint. Pours it in a glass, holds it up to my lips. "I can do that." It's a big glass. I have to hold it with two hands at first, but then I can do it with my right hand only, cookie in my left hand. "You want one?"

"I brought them for you."

"Go ahead and have some."

He takes out three of them, hand goes toward his mouth. "Hey!"

He puts two of them back, laughs. This ESPN is a joker. When we're done with our cookies, he says: "Well, Salt, what should we talk about today?"

Talk? I think I forgot how since Maggie's gone.

"Salt, where are you?"

I don't want to talk. Why did he come around anyway, Jerry's dick? A big guy, almost a fat guy, hardly fits on the little chair. He's wearing a suit today, blue suit and red tie, like he's a lawyer or a ward healer. I used to make deliveries to guys like him. Big shot lawyers with their offices in Manhattan and their boats out on Long Island. Have Salt bring over the compass—it's in the catalog, page twenty-four; have Salt bring over the Power Squadron uniform, the Captain's hat.

When I arrived, the secretaries would buzz back on the intercom: Commodore Nauticals is here. The big shots liked to come out front and give me the glad hand, just like I was one of them. Hey Salt, how have you been keeping yourself, how're they hanging?

"Maybe next time," ESPN Jerry's dick is saying. "I'll come around in a few days. We can just sit around and eat cookies or watch television. We don't have to talk."

The doctor came in and told me I couldn't have shots again, but I could have an IV drip with pain medicine in it. There would be a little button or something I could use to control it. This is because Yelena told him I was moaning and crying during the night. "I think he painful." The doctor always looks bored. I can see he's thinking why can't he be doing real medical stuff, instead of giving pills to old guys and listening to nurse's aides talking Russian in a nursing home. I think he likes being God around here, though. He says pills, you get pills; he says drip, that's what happens. For myself I like the shots best—Yelena or Gypsy or Millie shooting me up, and the good feeling when all of a sudden the medicine starts working.

The beings of fire come and signal to me. I always know which one is Maggie and which are her friends in the star world. Those few are always in front, but there are lines and lines of them, stretching far away, sometimes being taken back into the fire and then coming out again. Even Maggie gets taken back and I can't see her anymore, only the burning star. But her voice is there: Come on, Jerry. When are you coming? You know how impatient I am, how I don't like to wait.

Gypsy used to come around to clean the apartment and watch me while my mother was out. I can hear her voice in my head. *Woman sure loves that Russian Tea Room and them matinees.* Those two didn't like each other. But, without someone to baby-sit me, the Russian Tea Room and the matinees would be out. My father wouldn't replace Gypsy just because my mother complained. Their fights shook the apartment, rattled the windows. I went to my room, got out my erector set.

ESPN is back again, this time with a couple of donuts full of cream. He brings a glass of milk for mine, coffee for his. I haven't finished the Mallomars yet; there's still one left, which I'll eat later. "You have a job?" I ask him. "You show up here all the time—doesn't your boss get mad?" Though I could do the same thing when I worked for Commodore, make a delivery then disappear for a while. I liked to go to Chock full o'Nuts, get a donut and coffee and read the *Daily News* a little bit.

"I'm retired," he says.

"You sixty-five? You don't look it." His hair is black, but it's true that he's lost plenty up the middle.

"I'm fifty-nine."

"What did you used to do?"

"I was an attorney."

I knew it. "I only used a lawyer once. I was making deliveries on a bike, and some guy opened the back door of a cab and knocked me over."

"What happened?"

"By the time I paid the lawyer off and took care of the doctors, nothing was left. I got a bad knee out of it, it didn't really work right after that. When I met Maggie, I had a little limp. She thought I might have got it in the war."

"Maggie—was she your wife?"

I shouldn't have said her name. Dumb shit! I don't want to talk to ESPN about Maggie.

"Salt, it's okay. I don't want to pry into your life. Let's just drop it."

He puts his hand on my shoulder. Big paw—he could have been a pitcher with that paw. It looks like Allie Reynolds' big paw, when I got his autograph. Outside Yankee Stadium—my father was standing with me. I can't remember if we still had money then, or if my mother was still with us, or if Aunt Millie had already moved in.

"She was like my wife, but we never got married."

He looks like he wants to find out more about it, but he doesn't ask, just says: "I never got married, either."

Millie comes in. She wants to sponge me down, give me a little bath. I like it better when Gypsy does it. When Millie moved in, Gypsy left. We didn't need to have her anymore and, besides, we couldn't afford to hire anyone, once my father lost his job. ESPN says he'll wait outside, but I don't want him around at all when Millie's sponging me. I know if I don't keep talking, he'll go away.

"Does it feel good?"

She hasn't even pulled the curtain. Even if there's no one in the bed next door, I like to have it pulled. The door is open and anyone can walk in. "Close the goddamn curtain. How many times do I have to tell you?"

"Be nice, Mr. Perelman."

"Where is Gypsy—I prefer her."

"Could you turn over for me, Mr. Perelman? I don't know who you mean."

"Gypsy—the black one."

"LeToya, you mean? She'll be here tomorrow."

Millie stayed home to take care of me. When my mother used to be around, she hardly touched me at all, but Millie never took her hands off me. I liked it better when she hit me than when she cleaned my ears, or looked in the toilet to see what I did or scrubbed me in the bath. "Leave him alone," my father would sometimes say; but not very often because it always started a fight, and he couldn't afford to lose her—she was all he had left.

"Come on, Mr. Perelman. You have to admit it feels good."

I'm waiting to become fire. It's more than time already. Maggie made me promise that I wouldn't help the process along. You risk being cast into hell, she told me. I don't believe in God, but if she did maybe there's something to it. Maybe you see God when you dream. He's the fire.

Night comes and there's pain. I use the IV as much as it lets me. It works, but I can't sleep. Only a little. I can't find the fire. Maggie—where are you? Yelena comes in to check me, takes my wrist. She stares into space, her lips moving while she counts my heartbeats. I feel like my heart is going fast, but Yelena doesn't notice. "Okay," she says. I don't think she knows how to count very well. She takes a thermometer out and sticks it in my ear. Millie used to shove the thermometer up my ass. She liked to do it. She held my hand while we waited four minutes for the fever to register. I pretended she was my mother.

"Perelman alone," Yelena says. "Not worry. Tomorrow. Friend come."

Does she mean ESPN? How would she know if he's coming or not?

He doesn't come. ESPN comes and goes as he pleases. Why should he give a shit for me? Only Maggie cared for me. They put somebody in the other bed. A bad one—he talks out loud. Like there's someone he knows in the room. Sometimes he gets mad and sometimes he starts whining. I'd rather have what I have than what he has. Gypsy's here. She straightens up my bed. "Listen, Gypsy. That guy is driving me crazy."

"I'll put on the TV for you, Mr. Perelman."

There's nothing on television. It's a vast wasteland. She flips through the channels. A ballgame comes up—this must be a Saturday. The players hop around like frogs. I can't keep track of them. I used to be able to keep score. I took Maggie to a game. She watched me fill out my scorecard. "Jerry," she said. "You amaze me."

The guy in the next bed starts talking again. He thinks he's having a conversation with someone named Wilma. I can't stand it. "Shut up," I yell at him, but it doesn't do any good.

Gypsy comes back in. "Be cool, Mr. Perelman." She gives the guy a pill and me a pill. He starts snoring. I can't keep my eyes open, either.

Where's the guy? He's gone. They must have taken him out, maybe roomed him with another nut case. I hear ESPN's voice out in the hall. Before he comes in, I move over to the far side of the bed, pull the covers over my head.

"Come on, Salt. I know you're in there."

"Where were you, yesterday?"

"I'm sorry, Salt. There was something I had to do."

"What?"

"I had a board meeting that lasted all day. I'm on a lay board for the Catholic Church."

"You a Catholic?"

"Yes, I am."

Maggie was a Catholic, too. She thought about being a nun. But it was before she met me. She told me that after we got together, she never thought of it again.

"I brought you something," ESPN says.

It's cheesecake. I think I already had breakfast, but it doesn't matter. There's always a place in my stomach where I can put cheesecake.

ESPN is wearing a suit again. I ask him if he puts it on to see me, and he laughs and says no he just came from the morning mass. "Maggie used to go in the morning. She never missed one."

"You had a good marriage together, a Jew and a Catholic."

"Who said I was Jewish?"

He smiles. "Perelman?"

He's no dope, this ESPN. I knew some lawyers that were pretty dim. The lawyer for Commodore Nauticals was one. His sister was the owner's wife. Some guy in the Power Squadron slipped on the deck of his boat and sued Commodore because he was wearing our boat shoes. The lawyer made a big mess of it and it cost Commodore a bundle. The owner canned the guy, but then his wife walked out on him. "Hey Dick, are you married? Did I ask you that before?"

"I'm not sure. Anyway, I'm a bachelor. I always played the field and then, I guess, it was just too late."

"I met Maggie when I was fifty-two and she was forty-five. She said I was her last chance, sort of joking, but I told her lots of guys must've wanted to marry her, the kind of girl she was."

"You got a picture of her, Salt? Let's see what she looks like."

The picture is in the drawer of the table, right next to me. I check every day to make sure it's still there. I'm sure that Millie wants to take it, but so far she hasn't found out where it is. To ESPN, I say: "I don't like showing it around."

"I'm sure it would be all right."

It's still there. Maggie and me—her arm around my back and mine around hers. She's taller than me, I only come up to her eyebrows. This is at Coney Island—you can see the Parachute Jump behind us, a little blurry. Maggie's wearing shorts. She's a big girl. She's broad where a broad should be broad, I always told her.

"Terrific legs," ESPN says. "You don't mind my telling you that?"

"She was a chorus girl. She was in *Damn Yankees, Bye Bye Birdie, It's a Bird, It's a Plane, It's Superman* . . . I forget what else."

"That's all right, Salt. I saw those shows. I must have watched her perform."

I never saw her. I never went to shows until she took me. "After she couldn't dance anymore, she was a secretary at the radio and TV union, I forget what it's called, and I came to work in the mailroom, and we met." I don't feel like crying in front of ESPN. "We had twenty-two years together. After she was gone, I didn't know what to do with myself. I talked to her at night. Like the roommate I had, talking to Wilma. Only I didn't bother anyone, because no one else was there. Maggie is fire now—she asked to be burned. When I get out of here, I want the same thing."

"You want to be cremated?"

"Are you hard of hearing, Dick?"

He laughs at that. "I am, a little. But I heard that. Who else have you told?"

"I told Gypsy, and the doctor, maybe."

"Would you like me to check on it for you?"

"How much is it gonna cost me?"

"There's no charge."

"I heard that before."

"Really," ESPN says. "I'm a volunteer. I don't charge for anything I do here."

"Okay, then."

He gets up. "I'll tell you what. Before I leave, how about if I hang up Maggie's picture for you?"

"Somebody's gonna grab it. It's my only one. I had more pictures of her, but I don't know what happened to them."

"Don't worry, Salt," he says, "I won't let anyone take it."

He has a cardboard frame that he puts the photo into. It fits exactly right. This ESPN is really something, a mind reader.

"How about over here?" He hangs it on the wall next to my bed. If I look through the middle of my trifocals, I can see Maggie's face. "Tomorrow is Monday, Salt. I'll come in the afternoon."

I'm waiting to see if anyone else notices the picture. I hope that it's Gypsy who comes in. It's taking a long time. I like having Maggie on the wall. I'll bet that ESPN told all of them he'd sue the shit out of anyone who touches the picture. None of them will dare.

"Hey Mr. Perelman—is that you?"

Maybe I slept a little. It *is* Gypsy who came in. I think I'm getting to be a mind reader, too, from hanging around with ESPN all the time.

"Who is that with you?"

"Maggie—my wife."

"Nice looking woman. You were kind of a handsome dude yourself, Mr. Perelman."

"You think you could keep an eye on Millie for me, make sure she leaves the picture alone?"

"Sure I can. Now I'm going to fix your IV. Have you been using your pain medication?"

I don't know. I can't remember using it. If it means I'm getting better, I don't want to. Maggie has been waiting for me a long time. I shouldn't be late.

Time goes slow in this place, then sometimes it zigzags around, like a bug on the ceiling. I can't see Maggie in the dark, but I know she's there. "You can kiss me, Jerry. If you feel like it."

"Do you mean it?"

"Try me out."

I think I'll sleep a little now. I can't stay up as late as I used to.

They got another guy in the bed next door. They must have snuck him in during the night. This one's no talker—he hasn't said a word. Millie's in there working on him, behind the curtain. Who knows what she's doing? It can be anything she wants, if the guy can't talk. She likes being behind the curtain with people who can't fight back. She better not try it with me, though. Especially now that I've got ESPN on my side.

He comes with a paper for me. "You think you can sign this, Salt?"

"What is it?"

"It directs the funeral home to cremate your remains."

"Did they do Maggie?"

"Yes they did."

Okay, I'll sign. ESPN says both funerals were paid in advance, Maggie's and mine. When my turn comes, he says he'll make sure they burn me like I want. "I've brought you something, Salt." Actually, he brought two things—donuts and a CD player with *Damn Yankees*, original cast. We listen. "That must be Maggie singing now," he says. "Can you pick out her voice from the others?"

I think I can.

"Hey, what show is that?"

The guy in the next bed—he can talk after all. "It's *Damn Yankees*. My wife, Maggie, was in the chorus."

"Yeah?"

When I look again, the guy has rolled over onto his back, staring at the ceiling. It doesn't look like he's gonna say anything more. I know what that feels like, the way I was before ESPN showed up. Who sent this ESPN to me anyway? Maybe it was God. Maybe he's an angel.

"Hey, how come you're a volunteer for me and not for this other guy?"

"I picked you, Salt."

"Whad'ya mean?"

"There's an organization that matches volunteers with patients. Beth Jeshurun felt you were a good candidate for the program. I looked over the files of a few candidates and, when I chose you, the people here approved it."

The people here? I'd like to know who. Maybe it's Millie. I can see her writing things in my file. *I'm your mother now, Jerry. I want to take care of you.*

"Don't turn away from me, Salt. What's wrong?"

"I don't like people reading all about me."

He puts his big hand on my arm. Allie Reynolds hand. I let him. "I've learned a lot more about you from our visits than I did from the file."

"What kind of program is it, anyway? You trying to convert me into a Catholic?"

"No way, Salt."

"Then what?"

"Well . . ."

"Well?"

"It's for people who are dying."

"Dick—you're dying?"

No, he's not. I get it now. It's me. Gwen Verdon is singing: Whatever Lola wants, Lola gets. And, little man, little Lola wants you. Maggie used to play this record all the time. Sit me in a chair and dance around me. Doing Gwen Verdon's part.

"Maggie's calling me. She wants me to be fire."

"I know."

"Why are you doing this? What's the matter with you, Dick. You got nothing better to do?"

"I don't know," ESPN says. He's frowning. "We all think about dying."

"You got no one waiting for you."

"No."

"You're a Catholic, though. You're in good with God. He'll take care of you."

"You believe in God, Salt?"

"Nah. Not much. But I know that Maggie is fire. She talks to me. At night."

"Bullshit."

The guy in the next bed. He says one word every fifteen minutes. Maybe I should time him and have ESPN put a pillow over his head the next time he's due to talk. Not that I care what he says. The poor schmuck. I haven't seen anyone visit him—not so far.

ESPN sits down next to me, doesn't say anything more, just rubs my shoulder, like a massage. His hand feels warm. We listen to the music: Who's got the pain when they do the mambo? Who's got the pain when they go: uh. Who needs a pill when they do the mambo? I don't know who—do you?

I guess I have the pain.

"Hand me that, will you?" ESPN passes me the control for the IV, and I push on it, a few good squirts. It'll take a while to work, but by time the record is over maybe I can sleep.

ESPN has started coming every day, now. They all know him—Gypsy, Millie, even Yelena. Millie has started being nicer to me. She always pulls the curtain when she cleans me up, and she doesn't boss me around so much. She even straightened out

Maggie's picture once when it was hanging on the diagonal. I know why she changed her behavior. It wouldn't be any fun to get the shit sued out of you by ESPN. The pain medicine has been working real good. I get a lot of sleep and I see Maggie most times. We'll be together soon, she says to me.

My mouth is dry. I don't have to ring for Gypsy, because ESPN is here. There's a glass straw I sip with, while he holds the water for me. He's wearing his blue suit. "Is it Sunday today?"

"No, Salt, it's Wednesday."

"How come you have the suit?"

"I came straight from my AA meeting," he says. "I like to wear my suit to remind me it's serious."

"I never knew you were a boozer."

"I should have told you. It never came up."

"Is it real bad? You can't leave off?"

"Five years I have. Almost six."

"If you ever think you're gonna go back on, you can call me. I mean it."

"I will, Salt."

"Maggie had a friend went to AA. She used to call us up sometimes."

"What did Maggie tell her?"

"Life is golden."

ESPN looks at me. He's a little fidgety today. He keeps rolling his shoulders, like he's trying to get his jacket to sit right. "Do you believe that, Salt?"

I have to think about that one. There's pain, and there's pain medicine. Maybe the whole thing is not really golden—only silver. But once you get made into fire, then it's all different. Nothing hurts, and you don't have to think anymore. There's no other people, not really, only flames. Sometimes Maggie is one part of the fire and sometimes she's a different part. I don't know if ESPN can understand all that.

"When I'm fire—what'll you do with yourself?"

He laughs, shakes his head.

"Maybe you can volunteer for another guy."

"I don't know."

"You can ask Yelena. She's the one who comes in the middle of the night, when it really hurts. She'll know which guy needs a dick. You have to talk Russian to her. I can teach you a little. I want you to take the picture, Dick. Me and Maggie, put it on your wall. Don't let Millie get it. Hey, you got something sweet? I feel like it now."

"I'll see if they have something downstairs."

They already sent me a Rabbi. Orthodox, with a skullcap. He looked about twenty, best they could do. I understand you're a Jew, he said. Sure, as much as the next guy. Would you like me to read to you—a Psalm, or something from the Talmud? He's wearing blue jeans and a tee shirt. He's got muscles all over like Arnold Schwarzenegger. They must have a gym in the shul. Or, I can just sit with you, he says. Did Millie send you? He's shaking his head, but I wasn't born yesterday. Rabbi, I don't need you. If I want someone to read to me, ESPN can do it.

"I found a Mounds Bar, Salt. Will that do?"

I can taste it. So sweet. Half for me and half for Maggie. "Hey, Salt, are you okay, wake up." *You're close now, Jerry.* I didn't do anything myself, Maggie, I waited. *I'm proud of you, Jerry.* "Salt? God dammit, LeToya, get the doctor up here!"

That's ESPN, Maggie.

*What's he yelling about?*

I don't know.

# Scott Withiam
# Prophecy

Just wandering, he picked up a new trail,

which cut behind the unfinished ends of some back lots,

and somewhere in there kicked up and picked up an old whiskey bottle,

and then the trail spilled onto a neighborhood ball field

next to a church and didn't pick up again. He stood in what was foul territory or out
of bounds

and shook the bottle. Some flecks faintly sounded.

On the bottle reflected one of the iodine windows

of the new, plain-lined church; it chimed in, so to speak.

And behind that window, glowing, red votive candles huddled.

Upon what were they reflecting? Periphery, he thought: head-on, a wave of stimuli,

but a glimpse of something greater in the margins,

prophecy's tool today buried, except when exercised

in contact sports watched by fans off in the margins; exercised only on the playing field
to help see

an adversary's approach, to dodge before slammed,

as in whomever once swigged from the bottle.

He held it up, tipped it toward him, peered into it. What about some fix

on the unknown? Out of nowhere, the big guy stormed out

on his front porch, from across the street screamed,

"You know better than to drink that shit here, asshole. Take it somewhere else."

# Sweet William

The book on gardens is inconclusive, in the margin maintains that

A battle rages concerning the origin of the plant's name: Saint William

Of York versus Prince William Augustus, the Duke of Cumberland versus

William the Conqueror. I have my own

Entry:

The book is right on one count: it

Will fill in quickly. One morning, a stranger's truck veers to the opposite shoulder (and

Speaks?), glances off a boulder, flips but lands right side up in a ravine.

Following some other trajectory in time—

A nice feature with plants,

Unless they spread too close to your house. I couldn't get out. I was first on the scene

As the driver slid out bloody and stunned. I was on my way to the abortion,

That kind of occurrence,

Nobody believes. There he lay. To be reminded,

And then to see how many others passed, because they couldn't see the accident below, while *I* urgently waved for anyone else

To stop. Of all things or occurrences,

A laundry truck pulled over, and without hesitation—

At its best—

Shrink-wrapped bundles of bleached towels headed for a university were spilled

To cover him. Plant. Clean, but nothing delicate about it

Out there. He shook from shock. I asked him his name. "Bill," he said.

Not *William*, more highly regarded.

He blubbered, "This isn't the first time this has happened."

"Shh, shh," I said, "it doesn't matter." What matters is that you're alive."

I had to get going. I had to make that appointment.

# World Retrieval

In front of the shouting gallery at the country . . .
at the county fair, one man, who was done shooting, shouted,
"Unfair!" He stood, fist raised, on the peopled side of the counters
and booths, among those strolling the alley of . . . *cats,*
*strays and gimmicks, alley of gamble, gambol* . . . "Fuck you,"
the argument began. What the hell was it called—
where we stood—*a gangway, walking the ___? Plank? A blankway?*
He had, the pissed off man said, shot it out, all of the red [of the target],
and he didn't get his prize. "Don't go here," he said,
of the shooting gallery, to everyone gallerying. *Don't go here,*
I thought, considering one word, all of it hinged to humankind's inabilities
to get the world right. Regardless, people kept right on lining up
and firing. *A promenade . . . du Lemonade, aisle of kitsch?* More
mongers and hangers-on milled, wanted blood.
And they were going to get it, unless I got the word right.
"They won't give you a prize."
"I gave you your money back. Have a nice day;
now move it along, dipshit. I said, *move it!*" Here it was—*the* moment.
*Midway*, that's what it was called, where we stood. Still,
the two guys, faces red and shot, inched dangerously closer.
And the overheated stoned fried dough guy ogled the mother
breast feeding. And her red-faced baby struggled

to get his head right. Then all of us stood wanting, but wouldn't you know it,
that's when the gates to the Demolition Derby opened.
Anyone swept up was swept inside. Inside there, the word changed.
No one saw no foreign makes—not made well enough
to take a hit. And the question was, How could you sleep,
if you drove one—with so much concern for the vulnerable areas—
rear radiator, front axle, say—where, if you got turned, or backed up
wrong, and then rammed, disabled, rammed again, could get flipped,
left hanging upside down, your neck snapped and at a total loss for words,
and then where might you be?
Well, we all got some cold water thrown on us.
The derby track was slicked so to keep down traction, therefore speed,
therefore keeping us safe. A giant watering truck did the job.
It hosed us off by accident. It was a hydro-seed truck in its real life.
In ours, we grew hair instead of grass. We went from green to red,
produced far more blades per square inch than advertised,
could get walked along, all over. It's also called the fairway.
Mostly, engulfed.

POETRY

# Tomaž Šalamun
# The Longing for Madness

*Translated from Slovenian by Michael Thomas Taren and the author*

When we moved across the valley, I lost my racket.
I can't play tennis without my racket.
I looked back to see those flat stones.
Water carried it.
When we moved across the valley I lost my bowl.
I won't pull down any wall any more.
Instead of the bowl I'll have to use
my head, it hurts.
My head is black.
On the potatoes there're blue butterflies.
Why don't they pick up those potatoes on the field?
Potatoes are not even a plinth for sculpture.
I have three swords.
All four sides of the world are black.
All four sides of the world crawl into a red
velvet bowl which drowns to the bottom of the sea.
I was killed by the light of Sinbad the Sailor.
I'm gum and iron.
Pears fall on my head, but I don't sense them anymore.
I tore the lower throat of the wolf.
I carried logs of wood on my shoulder.
Then I met the Little Husk.

Algae grow in the Andes.
Don't give tips.
A pail of iron is more valuable then a pail of gold.
Always greasy hands turn the page of the paper.
The mountain chain slips from the frogs' backs.
Jade is inside.
I don't have blood, I have jade.
These are intrigues of letters-peseros
functioning as the agents of genetics.
Blow the cotton wood from your code!
The cotton wood doesn't subsist in paradise.
In paradise the bell subsists
thundering to the ground,
so the platform brakes.

# Miners

Palms burn.
Palm trees burn.
Triangles burn.

A horse paws on the sand like a girl from
the north touching nettles.

Gold caves open.
Water freezes.
God's eye swills little brooks
and blows on the heart.

Fog rises from leaves.
Someone in an apron runs accross the porch.

The whip bursts.
The sun falls.

# Eagle, Squirrel, Doe

Mama, I rob.
I ground my pretzels, brothers.
I gave away all my words.
The rose in me rises,
palpates, pulls tight the sweet mass,
caresses, caresses the stone.

You're hugged.
Water trod down
what was to be trodden down.
O ox ball mushroom,
the wound mediatrix.
Bricks, don't contract.
There under the deck, they still burn sailors.

And you: eagle, squirrel, doe,
triangle of all relations, all things:
you're both of us.
Ours are all these white pearls in the sky,
in your sweet, set wide night.
I cut you into your mouth.
Into the cross.

# 12 October 1980

The little silver fish showed up first.
They swam in a mass that was a cross between
milk and sky. I knew it would ring
if I hit it. I didn't hit it. I didn't even
touch it with my eyes. First green wheel
started to tumble, then the brown one, then
the grey one. Everything was missing. I was
totally cynical. I went to shit in the middle of a vision,
to shave and put on Givenchy. The wheels were
being carried, they weren't turning. They were forming
a triangle, which hurt for lack of a fourth.
Fish moved like stars, like a thousand
sperm on a negative. Faces began.
Cyclopes in fog. In their eyes burnt red
bushes. An old man's body buried in
something transparent and yellow. His face
was brown. Wheels began to turn and
hiss, and it smelt nice, but smells
give me away. I flushed. And again,
because it didn't flush the first time. I began
to shiver. I made sure the woman wouldn't look at me.
I stretched out my hands. The hands turned to

tulips, a sign for me to defend
my culture. Red tulips became green
with swords drawn on their petals.
They were plucked and taken. Fish let this
go undisturbed. If the fourth wheel is missing,
everything is missing. Massacres are between three and four.
Elohim has no right in my dome. Four is
a city, three is eternity. I don't want to be an inhabitant
of anything. If the fourth wheel appears any time but now,
I will be strangled and killed, mangled and,
at best, only a cell of another
body. Like titanium compounded with aluminum.

# Eli Rosenberg
# So It Goes

It was two-thousand and ten years after Jesus was born and twenty-three percent of students thought Spider-Man was as real as Winston Churchill. This was quite surprising to teachers who remembered teaching World War II to their students, but not Marvel Comics. After all, Churchill had been instrumental in defeating the most evil villain in the world while Spider-Man only fought imaginary bad-guys and tried to work up the confidence to kiss his girlfriend.

Recently however some people said that Churchill was actually a bad-guy, because he ordered many bombing raids on civilians in Germany. These people said that World War II was maybe not that necessary after all. Seventy-million people died, most of them civilians, some of them bombed by Churchill's airplanes, and it had not ended wars for good as many people had thought.

Most could agree that Spider-Man was a hero however, with the exception of Venom, Dr. Octopus, and the Green Goblin[1] who were hell-bent on his destruction. This was because they were villains. Children at school called Spider-Man a nerd which was an insult because Americans did not like nerds. The children did not know he had super-powers. Spider-Man did not hold it against them and would still save them if they needed saving. He was a hero and a bookworm.

People did not read comic books any more, although old ones with titles like *The Return Of the Fearsome Fly* and *How Green Was My Goblin* could be bought on eBay and at specialty shops for hundreds, sometimes thousands, of dollars. Americans did not read as much as they used to and if they did they bought what-

---

1 The Goblin's 'greenness' was both literal and metaphorical.

ever Amazon.com had recommended especially for them. Other people read replicas of books on small electronic tablets. To many, this was a sign that the written word could triumph in the changing times, although others pointed out that you could only pick books from a list chosen by someone else, that you could no longer read while basking in the sun, nor could not give such a book to a passing traveler once you were done; after all these books did not really exist.

Some people said that the average American reader who had time to read twenty-five books a year in 1945 only had time for four now, even with these electronic tablets. Many bookstores went out of business. A lot of people said that the decline of book reading represented the death of knowledge itself and was a sign that the culture was devolving. Others said that the novel was an archaic form of entertainment and that new genres like blogs, flash fiction, hypertext, and even html code were the zeitgeist and more attuned to the demands of the day.

It was sixty-five million years after the dinosaurs had died and people were in the habit of saying things were dead, over for good, or completely exhausted and used up. Hip-hop was often proclaimed dead, while others said that it was never alive. Jazz had bit the dust a while ago. Newspapers were undoubtedly on their deathbed. CDs were definitely six feet under. The American auto industry had dug its own grave. Academics said that the exhaustion people felt was a result of the many wars and choices inspired by capitalism. They called this postmodernism, although many people said that postmodernism was dead also. Death was not dead however, at least not in the year 2010. Some people said human contact was dead to the person sitting across from them at the café. Other people said that romance was dead, but that was because they were cynical.

It was true that people were finding new ways to connect to each other. People wrote instant messages, text messages, emails, and made phone calls more often. Other people posted quick updates about themselves on websites so that other people could see what they were up to without even having to phone. I'M DOING THIS RIGHT NOW, these messages often said. On any given day many people were undoubtedly having the BEST DAY EVER.

Other people sent pictures to each other and videos with little messages like ISN'T THIS FUNNY? Often, it was very funny. At concerts people held up their cell phones instead of their lighters, and sometimes they called a friend first. Some people took videos that they would later post to a website. Other people went on vacation and when they saw a beautiful sunset, would do nothing but take pictures of it until they had the perfect one. Then the sunset would be over but it would live forever on their camera and they could relive the moment at home with their friends who had not been there at the time.

# It was sixty-five million years after the dinosaurs had died and people were in the habit of saying things were dead, over for good, or completely exhausted and used up.

It was ten years since a man from Texas became president and the Americans had elected a new president. The New President was very hard to label or categorize. His father was an African from Kenya and his mother was an American from Kansas, so it would not have been wrong to say he was African-American. For a long time people debated whether he was really black or not, after all he was not descended from slaves and his mother was white and he spent much of his early life on various islands in the Pacific Ocean. On the other hand, he liked to play basketball and listen to rap music and he even had an Afro once. The debate raged on.

After he was elected everyone forgot about these questions and agreed that he was United States' FIRST BLACK PRESIDENT.[2] Many people were very excited about this; a homeless man walked around Manhattan chanting PAINT THE WHITE HOUSE BLACK and the NEW YORK TIMES declared that RACIAL BARRIERS HAD FALLEN and even the man from Texas said it was a MOMENT OF HOPE AND PRIDE for all Americans.

It was one hundred years since the first state adopted the ONE-DROP RULE and race was still a contentious issue in the United States. Some people said that the election of the New President was proof that racism was dead, while other people said that it was proof that it never really existed in the first place. Academics liked to show how race was a social construct, a way of categorizing people into boxes in which they did not fit neatly or tidily. A few people said we had entered a POST-RACIAL ERA, whatever that meant, and one man in particular told a pollster in rural Pennsylvania that he was VOTING FOR THE NIGGER, the day before the presidential election.

It was true that where you and your family came from was important to the person you turned out to be. But it was also true that if you walked from the Iberian Peninsula, through Europe and the Middle East, all the way to the bottom of Africa

---

2 The FIRST AFRICAN-WHITE-BLACK-HAWAIIAN-AMERICAN PRESIDENT, more accurately.

five hundred years ago, even back up into Asia if you had the energy, it would have been very hard to determine where one race stopped and another began, the various tones all blending together with the color gradient of a giant box of crayons.

It was three hundred and eleven years since the wall on Wall Street was taken down, and most people agreed that the United States economy had seen better days. Many economists said it was the WORST ECONOMY SINCE THE GREAT DEPRESSION, while others argued that it was merely a SLOW-DOWN and people who were really frustrated called it an ECONOMIC SHITSTORM. Many people lost their jobs and they certainly felt shitty. Other people could no longer afford to fly to Paris for the weekend or drink vintage Bordeaux or shop at nice stores on Fifth Avenue, and they felt depressed and slowed-down. A lot of stores and companies went out of business and many important banks and firms had to be rescued by the government. During the holiday season, a crowd chanting PUSH THE DOORS IN outside of a Wal-Mart early on the morning of a big sale stampeded a worker to death after doing what they said.[3] There were still many people who made a lot of money just by making money, but there were many more people who ran out of money because nobody wanted them to make anything anymore.

Other people said the poor economy was a result of a deficit of over a trillion dollars rung up by the government for a few very expensive wars. The two wars the United States fought cost over nine hundred billion dollars and counting, over six thousand dollars per taxpayer. If you can't tell, that's a very large amount of money, enough to double the amount of elementary school teachers in the United States for five years, or build a mansion for every homeless person or let every high school student go to college for free or take everybody in the world to Disneyland for not one, but two whole days.

For a while people couldn't decide what to call the Iraq war. The media began by calling it an INVASION, then settled on WAR and eventually moved to QUAGMIRE. The US Military referred to it as OPERATION: IRAQI FREEDOM, but people at protests thought it was more of an OCCUPATION. The man from Texas stood on an aircraft carrier a few months after the war began in front of a banner that said it was a MISSION ACCOMPLISHED. IRAQ IS FREE he proclaimed, MAJOR COMBAT OPERATIONS HAVE ENDED. At the time of this speech only one hundred and thirty nine American soldiers had died in Iraq. Since then more than four thousand American soldiers and countless[4] Iraqi citizens have lost their lives.

---

3 It is no good to be a person of your word if your words are no good.

4 Most estimates fall between 1 and 1 million.

The Iraq war was started because the man from Texas said that the ruler of Iraq had weapons of mass destruction. It is estimated that the United States has at least four thousand active weapons of mass destruction. After the invasion, it was estimated that Iraq had zero weapons of mass destruction. Other people said that the United States went to war because the Texan wanted to avenge his father's loss in the first Gulf War. Similarly, Spider-Man had decided to become a superhero because someone had disrespected his father also,[5] going as far as killing him. The Texan did not have the ability to climb walls and shoot webs however. People disagreed about whether he was a hero or not.[6]

The war took place in Iraq, a country in what the Western World calls the Middle East, archaeologists call Ancient Mesopotamia, and anthropologists call the Cradle of Civilization. After the invasion, many of the country's archeological and architectural heritage was damaged or destroyed; the ancient ruins of Babylon were taken over and turned into a base camp with tanks and a helipad, the ziggurat of Ur marked with gunfire and shrapnel, and the Lyre of Ur, quite possibly the world's oldest musical instrument, looted from the Iraqi National Museum and found broken into pieces.

The United States constitution states that the country cannot officially declare war without Congress's approval. Yet the United States had fought many wars since the Second World War, somewhere between four and forty depending on who is counting, and none of them had been approved by Congress. They did not approve the war in Iraq but they approved the spending, and many people said it was the same thing. At some point people stopped being so concerned with the war in Iraq and what to call it and the New President ordered the troops to Afghanistan, where the war continued. Apparently wars could move around.

It was one hundred and nine years after oil was discovered in Texas and Americans drove more than any other people on the planet. There were more cars than people over the age of eighteen in the United States. Some people drove big cars that needed many gallons of gasoline, often by themselves. Other people drove cars with bumper stickers that said REDUCE AMERICAN DEPENDENCE ON OIL, also by themselves. Some people drove hybrid cars that did not make very much noise and could go much farther distances with the same amount of gasoline. Americans were increasingly aware of their carbon footprints because the rate at which they consumed resources and produced waste was thirty-two times that of the developing

5 Peter Parker was actually an orphan who did not know his real parents, but he was adopted by his Uncle Ben, whom he considered a father and who was killed by a villain.
6 He was not a hero.

world. They did this by eating a lot, driving frequently, and enjoying the AC. They also bought many things that they stopped liking after a year or two. It was said that if everyone ate like the Americans did the world would need at least three and a half other planets to grow food and raise animals. Luckily everyone did not eat like the Americans did. Many people did not have very much to eat however and they did not feel lucky.

It was 4.6 billion years since the earth was formed and many scientists said that it was getting hotter because of all the carbon that was burned on earth was put into the atmosphere. These scientists remembered such axioms as ENERGY IS NEITHER CREATED NOR DESTROYED and ALL SYSTEMS PROCEED TOWARD ENTROPY. They called these axioms the second and third laws of thermodynamics. Many people who were not scientists and did not know what entropy meant noticed that the summers were very hot these days, although no one could remember if that had been true for a while. And some people said that global warming was a hoax, or that it happened periodically and was in no way irreversible. Some people even looked forward to the warming of the globe because they did not like the cold very much.

It was fifty-six years since the first color TV broadcast in the United States and it was said that wars had turned into simulation because it was experienced by the public only as a media spectacle. People were wowed with the shock and

**Now a person could sit in a shack near the Caribbean and instant message someone in Jerusalem HEY FRIEND, MY FEET ARE IN SAND THAT PIRATES WALKED ON MANY YEARS AGO, and they would not be lying.**

awesomeness of it, broadcast live on FOX, CNN and MSNBC. Children could play a video game called FALLUJAH: OPERATION AL-FAJR named after the military's OPERATION: AL-FAJR in the real Fallujah.

It was one hundred and thirty-four years after the first words were spoken through a telephone and many people got telephone calls about credit cards from people who spoke English with funny accents. And if they asked where this person was calling from, the caller would say a place like Mumbai or Delhi. And if they said I'M NOT INTERESTED IN A CREDIT CARD BUT I AM INTERESTED IN

MUMBAI the person would say WE WELCOME YOUR VISIT SIR and get off the phone very quickly. These callers were very nice but very busy.

The world was still an interesting place, and now a person could sit in a shack near the Caribbean and instant message someone in Jerusalem. They could write HEY FRIEND, MY FEET ARE IN SAND THAT PIRATES WALKED ON MANY YEARS AGO, and they would not be lying. They would not be pirating either unless they were downloading illegal music or stealing someone's treasure.

It was thirty-eight years after the first movie with oral sex was shown in American theaters and Americans spent ten billion dollars a year on pornography and nine-and-a-half billion dollars a year on the movies. Marijuana, which young people called WEED or CHRONIC and their parents called GRASS, and Jamaicans called GANJA, was now the biggest cash crop in the United States. This was called a black market transaction because it was supposed to be conducted underground or in the dark. Westerners had been afraid of darkness in all forms since the Romans, who used the word DARK to mean BAD because their slaves had darker skin. These days some people were so comfortable that they made black market purchases in the light.

Many tacos were sold illegally and tax free out of trucks in Los Angeles and other cities with large Mexican populations. The city with the second highest number of Mexicans in the world was not Guadalajara, Puebla, or Monterrey, but Los Angeles. The most Mexicans in the world however lived in Mexico City which was home to some twenty millions of them. The tacos in Mexico were very good,[7] but many people still immigrated to the United States every day. Some of these people who entered the country illegally also ended up selling tacos illegally. They were often darker skinned than most Americans and many people thought black market activity by these darker-skinned immigrants was bad.

It was four hundred and fifteen years after Shakespeare wrote *Richard II* and people were increasingly concerned with how they would be remembered. Some people imagined their funerals. Other people sought to make up for past wrongs. The Vatican apologized to Constantinople, which is now called Istanbul in a country called Turkey,[8] for the sacking of the city by knights during the Fourth Crusade eight hundred years ago. Villagers in a settlement called Nubutautau in Fiji wept and apologized to the descendants of a British missionary who was killed and eaten by their ancestors over one hundred and thirty years ago. Apologizing and making

---

7 They are made with fresh tortillas and avocados.
8 Turkey is an ancient country that has no connection to the American holiday Thanksgiving.

reparations for past wrongs was very popular. This way, people felt they were finally absolved and could do as they pleased without feeling guilty ever again. For some reason history made people feel very guilty.

It was 1,388 years after the prophet Muhammad emigrated from Mecca to Medina, and history was increasingly a point of contention. Many people had different ideas of what happened in history, like whether humans lived at the same time as dinosaurs or whether the Holocaust happened or whether the Atomic Bomb needed to be dropped on both Hiroshima *and* Nagasaki. Many Americans liked to see history as an unbroken line of great progress, like a graph that just kept getting higher, always approaching but never reaching the limit.

Many scholars agreed that history was difficult to understand because it was so full of pain and suffering, like a tragedy on repeat.[9] Some said that history was a continuum and others said that history was really a möbius strip and someone else wrote that history was a gorgon: stare at it too long and you'd turn to stone. A few said that all history was constructed because it only existed in written words and what did words mean anyways?

It was a few thousand years since Jesus was born and the Americans continued eating and sleeping and talking on cell phones. They typed and played sports and watched TV and took pills. They argued and debated and got angry with each other. They dropped their kids off at soccer and they made dinner for them and they rented *Spider-Man 2*, which was better than the first. They sat in traffic and they talked about the weather and they watched the ballgame. They laughed and cried and made love and got sleepy. The world spun wildly on its axis. And the people said many things.

---

9 Would it be Shakespearean or Greek? Or maybe tragicomedy? Are we the villains or the heroes? Do we even have a choice? Is there someone writing the lines for us? Would that make them the villain? Or do we all have minor roles, so inconsequential that we can say whatever we'd like in our brief moment on stage? Would you rather be Iago or Othello? Mustardseed or Macbeth? What if nobody came to the play? Wait, no wait, what if the show was rained out . . . FOREVER?? Does the producer give rain checks? Maybe he has a big tarp? Your call on all these.

# Weston Cutter
# Flinch

We're talking chin music, talking step
   back, talking you're in too close or
someone on your side made problems
   recently but you're the one who will hit
the dirt for reasons of what place you call
   home: we were watching the video of
the man chasing the daughter chasing
   the brother chasing the dog, wife framed
in window, and my love turned and asked
   *What's the flavor of her disappointment?*
before she'd wondered aloud what a girl
   had to do in her own home to get her
man to pick up his goddamned boxers:
   and now finally dinner, finally most of
the goddamned boxers picked up and
   we'd once again begun talking but failure
is looking at a steak you've made for your
   love knowing it's not enough: and though
we'd kissed only an hour earlier
   I heard a whistling and flinched

# Exposure to Various Flow

FOR JOHN HALTER

*Five to the good*, we'd say into radios, the Mississippi filthy, aswirl
            and sunflinty all around us, *five wide* we'd tell the captain
back in the pilot house as he ushered the barge half-blind
toward the dock slowly. There was a line, a piling, green steel
we knew to aim the boat toward kissing. *Four and a half.*
            From the deck Minneapolis stood sunlit, picturesque
                        as a thin-dressed woman behind us and we ached
            to unzip so much, and we floated north in a neighborhood
it was a crap-shoot to bike through past dusk. *Four wide.*
Different captains wanted different widths,
            maneuvering dependent on weather, wind. The best scenario
was dead-on, breezeless, *coming in on the line*, the barge's star
                        -board corner aimed to connect
            like a slow-motion prize-fighter's face with the punch
                        of the piling. Oddest was how we out there,
bow's edge, were the nervous ones, watching, while the captains
            breathed deep, moving through other currents. Wind
coming one way demanded one steering, the other way
            another: you aimed for the bad or good and counted on wind
to correct things in the last seconds. *Three to the good.* The difference
            between coming in bad or good was where the boat was aimed
            to blind-man-touch the dock and the difference

between us 19 year olds out on the boat's guard-
      rail and the captains we anxiously talked into the dock was weight,
      exposure to various flow, ability to steer 93-ton barges against
and into spring-flood-fed running water or wind. *Foot and a half*
*to the good.* The difference was that none of us on those boats's edges
had taken our loves up to the top floor of any of those skyscrapers
      whose reflections we floated past + boated through—
the difference was the captains had,
and did, and while we'd talk kissing and bases the older men
would laugh at us and, arms across their chests, kindly not tell us
what we didn't know. *Foot wide.* The best times were easy like
falling, like drinking that fourth beer: inevitable as a perfect
first kiss, or last kiss, or whichever kiss it'd be that let us know
which girl we were supposed to take to those floors and buy dinner for.
We painted our limbs onto the horizon's darkening blue,
      threw heavy rope at metal and hoped it took. *Line on.* The captains
couldn't see the corners we stood on with our radios and lifejackets,
we couldn't've driven those boats, and we never said it but all hoped
someone was watching, would see our cinema, how gently
we could, with effort (rope on metal, river's current read), guide.

# R.A. Allen
# Monday Burning

I suppose you could call it a busman's holiday: I'm a liquor salesman for Tri-Star Distributors, and this is a bar called Mike's Place, and I'm taking the afternoon off. Mike's is not a dive, exactly, but it's not the Oak Bar, either. Because it's on the edge of a neighborhood, some folks might call it a neighborhood tavern. On the other hand, they might just as easily think of it as a has-been version of the trendy watering hole it once was back in the seventies, back when it was called something else. I doubt, though, that many people give the definition of what Mike's *is* this level of analysis. But I have to. I have the account for their well liquors, the stuff they pour in your glass when you don't care enough to specify a brand.

I survey all that lies before me, which is not much, it being a Monday in the middle of the afternoon. Besides me, there are a couple of guys at the bar. The new waitress is taking an order from a six-top of seniors. There's an artsy young couple at another table. They appear to be stoned. I look for the owner of the biker bike that is parked outside, but I don't see a person that would fit that description. Maybe he's in the john. The fat guy who is always here on Monday is sitting alone at the same table in the far corner, smoking his cigarettes, reading a book, and drinking whatever it is he drinks out of a snifter. Cognac? Brandy? This place isn't classy enough to carry Armagnac. The Zaff twins, known mostly as The Power and The Glory, are tending bar.

My lovely companion is Joyce; she's a waitress here. Between studying my surroundings and holding this glass so that the scotch will stay inside and patting through my pockets for another pack of smokes, I've completely missed the last five minutes of what she's been saying to me.

"You're not even listening to me," she complains while roughly nudging my shoulder. But she's good-natured about it due to (A) we are old friends, and (B) she's used to it because most people find her boring. Joyce and I have had casual sex throughout the years and still do when it's convenient. For us, it's as normal as having a drink now and then. Sexual friendship—what could be more natural and comforting?

## An arm movement catches my attention. A glass whizzes past a bartender's head and smashes among the row of premium scotches on the back bar. Ricocheting ice cubes and an aerosol flourish of pink liquid complete the display.

The L-shaped bar is a long one, forty feet that run nearly the length of the room, plus ten more feet—the part referred to as the rocking chair—that make up the foot of the L. I always sit at the rocking chair. Down bar, a nattering disagreement is gaining volume between a customer in seersucker suit and The Glory. Leastways, I think it's The Glory—the Zaff boys are hard to tell apart from this distance.

"—told the clerk that I didn't *want* kumquats, I wanted kiwis," Joyce is saying.

I give her a sympathetic nod. We all need a little validation now and then.

An arm movement catches my attention. A glass whizzes past a bartender's head and smashes among the row of premium scotches on the back bar. Ricocheting ice cubes and an aerosol flourish of pink liquid complete the display. Notwithstanding the dissipated lifestyle of bartenders nearing thirty years of age, the twins are quite athletic; The Glory (or is it The Power?) manages to grab the unruly patron's offending arm by the coat sleeve. The Glory's other hand forms a fist that pops the guy across the bridge of his nose. The guy retaliates with his free arm, but the blow glances off The Glory's shoulder. Ashtrays, Bevnaps™, drink coasters and anything else on the bar within reach of the combatants goes flying. With piston-like jabs, The Glory whacks the guy's face and head.

The males among the table of seniors stand up to better see what is happening. I head for the action.

Joyce grabs my arm and forces me back down. "Stay out of it," she snaps. "You're too drunk and too old. Bump!" she yells, searching for Bump, a large Negro who cooks in the afternoon and bounces at night. "Stay put," she orders me, and then dashes for the kitchen. The ease with which she's put me back in the seat of my barstool convinces me there is something to what she says.

By now, The Power has rushed to the aid of his brother, grabbing the guy's collar. The Power and The Glory attempt to pull him over the bar where they can inflict some honest damage, but their victim is having none of it. Firmly in opposition to their plan, he has rigidly angled his midsection at the bar's edge while bracing his knees against the front of the bar—not to mention he is also a fair-sized person. He mule kicks a barstool clattering across the room. The artsy couple goes, "wow," the fat man in the corner lowers his book.

From within the kitchen, I can hear Joyce shouting for Bump, who is most likely to be out by the dumpster smoking a joint.

I am surprised that, while the room is filled with the noises of human combat, most of the sounds are unintelligible. Rather, they are the guttural beginnings of words, their endings being lost in eruptive exhalations. The guy makes "k"-type grunts that I interpret as an attempt at "kill." "Muff—" is in there a lot, too.

The Power and The Glory still have him by the sleeve and collar of his suit coat, but one of the guy's arms is still free. Flipper-like, it flails viciously, still capable of destruction. The twins' punches are landing more haphazardly now. The Power throws a hook that hits the guy on the top of his head; I see The Power wince at the pain in his knuckles.

Finally, like the Rock of Gibraltar on casters, Bump emerges from the kitchen, ducking his head beneath the doorway's lintel. Joyce is flitting around him on all sides like a mama bird, urging haste. Bump is the personification of menace, a movie version of the heavy who breaks arms for the mob. He grabs the guy by his belt, and, in a voice lower than the slippage of tectonic plates, tells the twins, "Aw' right, I got him now."

But the twins, deaf in the freight-train roar of their own adrenaline, are totally committed; they aren't even aware that Bump is in the same city. They have the guy secured by clothing, flesh, and hair; plus, for extra leverage, they each have a foot planted against the side of the beer cooler beneath the bar. He belongs to them.

There is a moment of equipoise, of stalemate, of impasse: two hyenas in a tug-o-war with a lion over the carcass of a wildebeest.

"Got him, I says," says Bump, hauling back.

Bump applies all 340 pounds of his bulk, and the guy then flies free of the twins' grasp. The guy looks like he's been sucked through a jet engine. Bemused, The Glory is left holding the unattached right sleeve of the guy's coat. Bump drags the goofa-loon to the front door and tosses him out on the sidewalk like a medieval housewife emptying a chamber pot.

I stand up, clapping and whistling and cheering for the twins and Bump—I have been grandly entertained. Joyce places her hand on my arm. "Baby," she coos, "we need to straighten you up. Come with me."

Again, I realize that she is right, and I allow her to lead me back to the store-room. On a tip tray, Joyce divides a mound of white powder into three lines with a credit card. She does one of them and then hands me a rolled bill, indicating for me to snort the rest. Which I do. My head clears immediately, and I show my gratitude by nuzzling and groping her. I put forth that a quickie amongst these fine boxes and crates might be salubrious. But, like a by-the-book cop, she eschews my attentions, citing a duty to employer and customers alike. She tells me to go back to my seat, have one more drink, and then go home to my wife. I tell her I will.

Back at the bar, The Power has his hand buried in the ice bin. It's swelling up on me, he says. The Glory is mopping up blood with a soda rag. I order my farewell scotch-on-the-rocks and settle in. The analeptic stimulant from the storeroom still courses in my bloodstream.

So: Am I an alky? It's hard to say. I know I drink more than the average moder-ate drinker, but it's not so much a need as a time management issue. What should I do? landscape my yard? take up golf? start a family? You see, the normal things haven't stuck to me like they do most people. Seven years of college; no degree. At forty-one, it's all I can do to maintain a marital relationship—and we're on our second trial-reconciliation at that.

The day nods back into its yawning pace, and everything is the way it was before all the excitement. One of the seniors wanders off to the restroom. I study the new waitress's posterior as she carries a fresh drink to the fat man in the corner. The Glory flips through the TV channels: soap opera, CNN, an up-in-arms talk show, soap, cartoons, baseball game. He settles on the ballgame. The Power mentions that he might need to go to the ER about his hand. The Glory calls him a pussy. No, really, says The Power. I nurse my drink and wonder what's for dinner—or if I'll be heat-ing up a can of soup. I like cream of mushroom. Do we have any? The minutes, like baseball innings, pass languidly—which is fine with me.

But then I hear a scream from one of the ladies at the table of seniors. The new waitress screams next, and I see a bright light. I see yellow-white flames in the corner. The fat man is on fire! Fire is all over him! He is already a charred silhouette within a sheet of flame from his waist to above his head. Every woman in the place is screaming. One of the old men is the first to take action by slinging half a pitcher of beer—which misses—at the burning fat man. The Glory, having located the fire extinguisher under the hand sink, vaults the bar and rushes to the scene. He aims and presses the lever but has neglected to pull the safety pin. "It's jammed, it's jammed!" he yells. From nowhere, Joyce appears with a tablecloth that she partially throws over the fire victim. The Power, now at his twin's side, yanks the pin; and, with a loud whoosh, a snow cloud of phosphate powder envelops the burning man. I dial 911 on my cell.

**I like cream of mushroom. Do we have any? The minutes, like baseball innings, pass languidly— which is fine with me.**

Amazingly, the smoldering, charbroiled fat man is still upright in his chair; he exhibits no signs of life. There is some residual smoke, but not as much as you'd think. Repellent as the sight is, everyone gathers around except for the artsy girl, who we can hear retching in the ladies room. Her boyfriend is taking notes on his forearm with a ballpoint pen. A nidorous stench hangs in the air, and our hands or our handkerchiefs or cocktail napkins cover our noses. We don't talk as much as might be expected, either. We just stare. I know what is dawning on us. We have all been party to a momentous, heretofore unwitnessed, phenomenon: Live Spontaneous Human Combustion.

The authorities arrive within minutes: firemen, then emergency medical techs, and then the cops. They shoo us out of the way, and a fireman with a tank on his back re-extinguishes the dead fat guy who finally falls from his chair. Somewhat uncertainly, the EMTs take over. After a glance at the corpse, the cops fan out amongst us, looking for answers. This is my cue to leave, and I drift toward the kitchen door.

It is apparently The Power's cue to leave, too, as he is also moving toward the kitchen. He says to no one in particular, "I need to go to the hospital."

"I'll drive you," I say. And we sidle unnoticed through the kitchen door.

In the lot out back, I ask, "Outstanding warrant?"

"Maybe," he answers. "What about you?"

"Maybe. Nothing serious, though."

"Me neither."

\*

At a nearby minor emergency clinic, it turns out that The Power's hand is only bruised, but he doesn't want to go back to his shift at Mike's, so I drop him off at his apartment and go home.

Boudica has one of her headaches. She's lying in the spare bedroom, lights off, and with a washcloth over her eyes. Normally, I know better than to attempt conversation at times like these, but I have just seen extraordinary. I *need* to talk about it. "Honey," I say, "you won't believe what just happened."

"Ummmph," she moans.

"This guy caught fire for no reason. He burnt like the Hindenburg, sweetheart, and—"

"Are you drunk?"

"No, baby. This guy just—right in the middle of Mike's, he just—"

"Have you been drinking?"

"No. Yes, but just two beers. He—this guy who's always there—exploded in a huge ball of fi—"

My wife flings her washcloth to the floor and turns on the bedside lamp and looks at me, her eyes crisscrossed with sleep and anger. "Does that whore still work there?" she demands.

"What whore?"

"You know what whore. The redhead with the boob job—Joanne."

"Baby, I don't know any Joanne."

"Not Joanne—whatshername, Joyce. *That* whore. You know who I'm talking about."

"I'da know. Yes. Yes, Joyce is still there. But this is not about Joyce or anyone who works there or the Queen of France. It's about a guy who—"

"You are such an asshole."

In my best frantic falsetto, I paraphrase John Hurt in his title roll of *The Elephant Man*: "I am *not* an asshole. I am a *human being*." I have used this one to defuse marital discordance before, and, at one time, Boudica would laugh and the argument would be over.

But not today.

She says, "Asshole bastard," and turns off the light and rolls to the wall.

Geez.

I love her, but we don't seem to fit anymore. Quietly, I shut the door and hurry to the kitchen. The evening news is about to air. There is no cream of mushroom, so

I open a can of tomato and shake its glutinous blob into a pan and put the pan on a burner.

With a heraldry of trumpets mimicking Morse code, the intro to Channel Six's *News At Five* brings the kitchen to life. The anchor guy greets us with the usual opening hello and all that. Incredibly, the lead story is about corruption at city hall, which, in this town, amounts to "dog bites man."

The next item is a murder: Unidentified male in his early twenties found shot in the head by nobody knows in a neighborhood populated by deaf blind people. All they show on this segment is a chalk outline cordoned off by yellow tape. Presumably, the ambulance left before the Channel Six van got there. They interview a cop who is "reluctant to discuss an ongoing investigation, but if any member of the public knows anything, they should come forward," blah-blah, "held in the strictest confidence," quack-quack, "cash reward for information leading to an arrest," et cetera, amen.

After the murder comes a report about a bus wreck—a school bus wreck. This is an attention-getter until you find out that there were no kids on the bus and that the driver was not hurt—not even a chipped fingernail—and that it was the bus that rear-ended a Volvo at an exurban four-way stop. I realize that this story is not about the wreck per se. It's about: if there *had* been children on board and if the wreck had been more serious, what then? Even the newscasters seem tired of it. I am astonished. Did this station somehow miss the event at Mike's altogether?

But then the pinstriped co-anchor says, "In a bizarre incident at midtown bar, a man burned to death. Witnesses say it was a case of spontaneous human combustion. Was it? Find out after we return."

And they go to a commercial—several, actually. I eat my soup and wonder about the fat guy. On weekday afternoons, he was always there in the corner with his book. Ordering drinks was the limit of his verbalization. He was the bar's mysterious stranger; nobody even knew his name. I wonder if he had people that he loved, people that loved him—like a wife.

On the sidewalk in front of Mike's Place, a reporter interviews a fire marshal in a crisp, gold braided uniform. He gives us the official account: Man catches fire, pronounced dead at the scene.

Now they cut, mid-interview, to one of the seniors who had apparently started out by trying to tell his life story before getting down to cases: retired mechanic, widower, moved down here from St. Louis in 1974 . . . . The reporter manages to rein him in. "We all looked up and he was on fire," says the senior. "He busted into flames. I tried to put him out with a pitcher of water, but the heat from the fire was too intense. It was instantaneous human incineration."

"Spontaneous," I say to the TV. "It was *spontaneous* human *combustion*."

Lastly, we hear from a spokesman from the Medical Examiner's office—scrubs, stethoscope, hospital badge. He tells us that the preliminary findings suggest the victim suffered a heart attack while drinking an alcoholic beverage, which spilled on his clothing and was ignited by a lit cigarette, thereby causing him to be consumed in fire.

"So, in your opinion, this was *not* a case of spontaneous human combustion?" prompts the reporter.

"No, it was not."

The co-anchor comes back on and tells us that the authorities are waiting to release the victim's name, pending notification of next of kin.

I turn the TV off and sag into my chair, deflated.

Now, I know a bit about liquor and can say with certainty that it won't ignite in a liquid state from contact with the heat of a cigarette. It's high school physics: when your waitperson flames your Bananas Foster on his tableside cart, he lights the preheated rum *vapors* rising from the sauté pan, not the liquid rum. I conclude that this medical examiner must not get out much.

I can't stay here in this too-too-quiet house; so, feeling obsessive and foolish at the same time, I decide to go back to Mike's Place.

After sundown, the personality of Mike's undergoes a metamorphosis of sorts. The crowd is edgier and it's too dark. Disparate groups of customers huddle together and give off sidelong glances while they hatch plots in low tones. It becomes the kind of bar that makes newcomers hesitate near the front door. I see that my usual seat is unoccupied. As I head for it, I look for veterans of this afternoon's fireworks. I don't see anybody except The Glory. He's been hooked into working a double shift, he explains when he brings me my scotch—goddamn night bartender no-showed. The Glory says that he is tired.

"Weird day, eh," I say, by way of starting a conversation.

"Too fucking weird. The brawls are bad enough, but puttin' out human torches is above and beyond the call. My nerves won't handle it. Thinkin' about getting outta this trade altogether, man. Many more days like today, and I'll go join a convent."

"You mean join a monastery, don't you?"

"Wherever they'll take me." And he heads back to the service bar to fill a drink order.

Through the darkness, like a figure stepping out of a Caravaggio, I see the artsy young guy from this afternoon coming toward me. He has longish, limp hair the color of black shoe polish, and he's dressed all in black and he wears a serious expression. (Some people are determined to stereotype themselves.) "Excuse me," he says. "Weren't you in here this afternoon?"

I allow that I was.

"Wow! I knew it. My name is Dirk."

(Dirk?) We shake hands.

He says, "Would you please tell my friends, here, what happened to the man that burned up." With him are a guy who shops in the same heroin-chic thrift store that Dirk does and another kid who is everybody's caricature of a computer dork. "I told them, but they won't believe me," he says. "And when the bartender backed me up, they think I put him up to it."

I say, "Guy attended his own cremation."

Suddenly, I am the standard-bearer of truth. His buds want details, and I give them. They ask questions, and I answer them. This end of the bar becomes the site of a lively conversation that's like popcorn popping in a bag. The Glory adds his comments when he is down this way. A couple that has seen the TV news overhear us and joins in. Somebody buys the next round. Somebody else plays devil's advocate.

Dirk tells me that he writes graphic novels, which I figure out are the same as comic books but not particularly funny. He and his friends are sci-fi enthusiasts, and they suspect a cover-up by the local authorities—a Roswell, a grassy knoll, a Watergate. Along these lines, graphic novelist Dirk is, at this very moment, gathering material for his next graphic novel. Can he quote me? Sure. Is it okay if he sketches my likeness into his work? Only if he makes me look like Clark Kent, I say, and we all laugh.

But it won't be another Roswell. It won't be anything. We're just people in a bar and nothing that ever happens in a bar is taken seriously the next day—even something like spontaneous human combustion. As a rule, I'm not the cynical type, but what I am experiencing at this minute is cynicism, and this makes me a little sad, a little sick. And I can't help from wondering about the dead fat guy.

The party continues, but I am outside the moment.

Down by the service bar, The Glory is doing exactly nothing. There is a lull in bar traffic, and he is simply standing there, gazing out at a nowhere void, mouth slightly agape. He looks beat. There is something else about him, though, something that gives me a turn. He seems to be glowing and fading away at the same time.

Oh, no, I am thinking, is he dying? Am *I* dying? Am I having a stroke? It's almost like I can see through him. Of course, it has to be a trick of the lighting in Mike's. His seemed transparency is probably caused by the fluorescent lights under the bar reflecting onto his shirt from the rippling dishwater in the deep sink. And the ethereal, bluish aura that appears to radiate from him surely has to be raining down from the TV or the neon clock, or perhaps it's from the back bar's illumination, smoky light-shafts fractured and prismed by the bottles that surround him. I blink hard a couple of times, and The Glory comes back into sharper focus. Whew, I think, we almost lost him.

One of Dirk's friends is asking if he can bum a cigarette. I hand him the pack. "Here, dude, keep 'em," I say. "I'm quitting."

# Doug Ramspeck
# Comfortable Life

I don't know. All this coming and going,
the snow at night beyond the city.
The scar of sky when we awaken
and stand at the windows. Across the street
there are cars in the funeral home
parking lot, and we pour a bowl
of cereal, and whatever happens we drive
to work and the hours are an argument
and so inscrutable. *Something fills the air
like desperate wings.* My hair has been shaved
close to my skull, and I awaken to the sound
of a bus or perhaps a barking dog. I pull back
the curtain and see the mourners arriving
in their cars, which means I am lonely
but in a way that seems for once
self-sufficient. It is either sad
or empowering to awaken here
these mornings on my own, and there's
a frozen river I walk to so I can recognize
the ice. I sit sometimes on this curb
and wait for you to walk by wearing

a woolen sweater and a red cap. It is possible
that when I stand to greet you
the snow will cling to us like ash.

# Gorgeous Light

We lived by a bay
that in the evenings
transformed to blood
and cracked my heart
like an alley full
of someone else's memories.

But as long as the sun
rose above the city,
as long as the sun set
behind the city,
we were bathed
in gorgeous light.

And when our child was born
his wails mixed
with the sounds of the buses
and the sirens.

You swore then that the moonlight
seeping through our windows
had its origins in the underworld,

that it spread like a strange fog
from the sidewalks and alleys
near the water.

It seemed to us that surely
someone had drowned.
How hard each day can feel.
You lift yourself and place
one foot before the other.

Then the buildings downtown
began disappearing from our lives.
Many days there was just the foam
near the shore, the gray and white birds
that rose and fell.

Or flew toward the city
and disappeared.

# Memorabilia

Someone died today.

You sit beside me
at the coffee shop.
Let's say we are made
of concrete and steel
and mirrored windows.
We close our eyes
and the city vanishes.

There are pigeons
fluttering on the street.
They used to be accountants
and shop keepers and lawyers.

We are waiting for permission
to stop pretending we are immune,
to grieve. To tear down,
if necessary, this city
stone by stone.

*In many a smiling mask*
*death shall approach beguiling thee,*
Whitman wrote,
and here the old man is today
walking in an alley
with the blowing snow,
while the great river
slows and seems to stop
by the bridge.
Nothing changes. Somebody
is laughing somewhere
and we talk in low voices
about the way a heart constricts.

The fact is that we carry
these deaths with us
in our pockets, in the way
our breaths form a mist
in the cold morning air,
and then we sip our sadness
from coffee cups
and hear the clink
of silverware around us.

Look: *here is another day.*
You have to think that.
Have to believe the sky has given
birth to it. That soon
you will walk out
into snow falling
from the sky as though
to cover everything.

# The History of Other Lives

Yes, you see it sometimes.
The great avenues
and stone buildings clustered
in strange filaments of light
amid the clouds. Ancient
and hidden, floating,
dragged on slow pulleys
across the evening sky.

Maybe you stop and light
a cigarette. Maybe
you have just come down the steps.
You hear the creak
of bus brakes or a siren
in the distance.

It's so sad: you watch the pain
of the lost city where you believe
that once you lived,
where no one lives
any longer. The emptied
streets and train stations
and park benches. The abandoned
glimmering of stilled cars.

Though tonight you dream
you are walking there.
Carrying yourself
like rag cloth. Carrying
yourself like an emptied husk.
Watching the earth being carried
on its great pulley
beneath you.

# Lina Meruane
# False Steps

*Translated from Spanish by Bernadette Walker*

—Why are you following me?

She had the voice of broken glass and she walked behind me, barely missing my heels with the points of her patent leather shoes. I thought she was teasing and turned around expecting to find a complicit smile. But I was met neither by smiles nor complicity: what I found was a girl with huge pupils, two black holes that blurred with her irises. Her corneas were irritated. And she seemed to never blink those eyes under the arches of two scant eyebrows. Her sparse hair looked coarse, her lips were chapped from constant licking. She never stopped biting them.

—I'm waiting.

She said, sending her mossy breath in my direction, the scent of the mornings when I crossed the yard on my way to school. It was the smell that emanated from her small body, from her clammy hands, from her bony fists, one clutching a sharpened pencil, the other a piece of paper. The smell of her breath was so intense that it seemed green to me, even though her tongue was perfectly pink, her gums red, her teeth white and a little crooked. Crooked like mine, which would very soon be perfectly straightened out by my braces.

She took a breath and dropped the ball of paper she had crunched up. She kicked it away, watching me with a hate that could have been fear. She was convinced that I was following her, so I turned back around and went on my way alone. She came up behind me, she dug a finger in my back, and I would have laughed if she hadn't then repeated herself, menacingly.

—I want to know why you are following me.

Her scent seemed even more intense once she quieted again. Or was it her pupils, the corneas crisscrossed by tiny veins. She was still clutching her graphite pencil, like a tool, with her other hand. I wondered if she slept near the canal, surrounded by watercress and weeds and wild flowers. But that was absurd: her body showed no traces of mud, the cuffs on her white shirt were impeccable, the bowtie on her uniform was spotless, and the elastic in her socks, unlike mine, held them firmly up to her knees. Her patent leather shoes gleamed, immaculate.

She jabbed me again with her nail, her sharpened index finger in the soft spot between my ribs and belt. An uncomfortable pain that would remain stuck there. Like the shards of her voice. Like her eyes. Hurting.

—My father told me to watch out for people carrying sacks.

I bunched up the burlap one I was carrying under my arm, trying to hide it behind my leather school bag.

—He also told me not to get distracted in school. The bogeyman could be a girl like you, with braces on her teeth.

I should have argued but I just nodded repeatedly, ashamed of my smile. I was imagining her in a sack, in my sack. Had she ever been in one, trying to move ahead by giant leaps? Was it possible she didn't have one, or that she'd never risked falling down, twisted up in her own legs? Had she ever skinned her knees? Her elbows? Did she know the thrill of stepping on the corner of a nearby sack to make her rival fall and leave the girl behind, defeated on the pavement? And if we were in the same school, why didn't I remember ever seeing her?

—Stop following me. You'll make me tell my father.

And she ran off, her skinny legs like two strings hanging down from her uniform.

Sunday, on the church steps, I sniffed the same scent of ivy, of lichen: an omen that stirred up my memory. That hint of green alerted me to the light footsteps very closely echoing mine. I guessed it was her shiny boots pausing with me at each step, until I stopped my ascent.

I was giving her time to start protesting.

—Why do you keep following me?

I took a deep breath, felt the cold air in my teeth.

—Do I need to tell you again?

I laughed as my stomach tensed and a stinging sensation went through my body. I hid my laugh, stood still, fixing my eyes on the trunk of a dried up pepper tree. I was still smiling when the church bells began to toll and five old ladies of varying sizes paraded rhythmically by me. They rushed down, fleeing their useless sins. I watched them disappear before taking another step and then waiting for her to close in. A few more steps up. When I was just slightly ahead I sped up four more, then suddenly halted. She did the same and came up even closer.

I noticed her gasp, short like a complaint.

I pushed the wooden door and followed along with the people who continued walking up, but by the time I had reached the altar she was gone. Only mossy traces of her were left in the air. I knelt to pray, still looking around in case she appeared.

My palms smelled strange, under the flicker of the candles I had the impression that they'd turned green. I took the rosary from my bag and fingering the beads, I said my prayers, including her in my petitions to the Virgin and the angels, asking that she reappear.

## Her scent seemed even more intense once she quieted again. Or was it her pupils?

For days I kept watch of the courtyard at recess and waited for her after school at the exit. My classmates walked by and stopped to question why I was waiting there, stalling, playing at tracing lines in the gravel with a stick. What was keeping me from going home, it was time to eat. Soon it would get dark. Night would come to fill us up with fear. But I just shrugged my shoulders, without losing sight of the girls sticking their heads out of the gate before running off home at full speed.

I never saw her leave.

I never saw her enter.

Maybe I'd mistook the tie and she was a student at another school, perhaps her father had forbidden her from coming or she was absent those days due to some illness. It didn't seem like a good idea to stay posted there; rumors were spreading, some of the girls had begun making bets: Was I waiting for a lover? Had I lost my mind?

And it was possible I would lose it, having to spend forty-five minutes straight, shut in a classroom, unable to look for her. My concentration was gone. Calculating a math problem became impossible. Putting together a sentence with a subject, verb, and predicate. Responding *present* when my name was called during attendance: absent. I could do nothing but go over and over ways to find her, to get her attention and make her understand: I wasn't following her, I never had. But how could I explain without seeing her? I was convinced that as I walked, my shoes were erasing her footprints, that we were passing through the same hallways at different times, that when I least expected it we'd run into each other at the corner. But when? Maybe, without my knowing it, our voices mixed together during the morning assembly hymn. Maybe we were breathing the same air. Maybe we bought the same snack at the stand, we ate from the same pack of cheese, the same baloney. I questioned the street vendor, the recess monitor, the guard. They didn't remember any student with sparse hair or black eyes with enormous pupils. Time was running out: summer was storming in, closing the school for vacation.

Two hot months shut in behind the window on the second floor. Nobody to play with, the freshly ironed sack folded over the chair, waiting for the race. The crashing of knees to the ground. The tumbles onto the cement. And Auntie constantly nagging: I should go out in the courtyard and take advantage of the cool morning air and the birds, I should venture out on the street, see if I could get some color, pale as I was. I needed to move around, get some exercise. I was withering. But I kept guard at the windowsill while the milk cooled in the glass and the jam on the bread collected flies, and my breakfast went bad. It all went bad: I couldn't open my mouth. Auntie would collect the untouched plates and grumble off to wash them.

I languished there staring blankly through the trees of the neighboring yard, down the nearby streets. My body felt full of air, of emptiness. Nothing more than a sour taste in my mouth, the plaque accumulating on my teeth. My head spun round at every little noise, I felt her hand touch my elbow, her nail between my ribs demanding explanations.

When would the summer end?

The bell began to ring while I was still a block away. I sped toward the other students already neatly lined up on the side of the assembly, and I pulled up behind the last one, breathless. All the girls had their hair long, pulled up high, all restless filly-tails, waiting for the start. We took in the headmistress's words of welcome in silence. Some girls turned to me and, mockingly, sucked in their cheeks to imitate how extremely thin I was. I shrugged off their teasing, and went on shining my shoes on the back of my calves as I carefully studied each head. I had not forgotten the shorn roundness, or her green scent; I knew it was only a matter of time till I once again felt a cool breeze carrying on it the smell of wet, rotting gardens.

\*

—You look emaciated.

The teacher leaned over me, pulling my bottom eyelid down to examine the inside. Too pale. She shook her head and sent me to the nurse with a handwritten note. The nurse looked at my nails, made me stick out my tongue, corroborated the possibility of anemia and sent me back to class with a letter for my aunt. It was a list of foods I had to eat every day without fail: raw spinach and chard and cooked broccoli and artichokes. Pistachios and beets too. And bloody beef. And if I felt weak or dizzy I had to go home immediately.

But I didn't feel tired, or even a little dazed. I was happy to be back, and I would stay at school as long as possible. In the courtyard, as long as possible. I'd take my time getting back to class, in case I was lucky enough to bump into her. The fragrance of freshly cut grass enthralled me along the way. The blast of fall wind at my nape made me shiver, it was a gust full of crackling leaves and steps. I stilled to see if she would approach, I waited for a finger to poke me between my ribs. Her whisper in my ear demanding that I quit following her, spying on her. She said that she had seen me watching her day after day from my window. When, she asked, breaking glass in my ears, when was I going to stop chasing her with the sack. I wanted to tell her that I had burned the sack. It was a lie. I was lying to her again. She would call her father. She was going to denounce me.

The guard appeared, upside down, lightly smacking my cheek. He blew on my face, and fanned air at the opening of my shirt at my throat. The trees held their branches over my head and the clouds came down and disappeared. I grasped at the blades of grass as he told me that the nurse was calling my aunt.

—Where is she?

I mumbled. My tongue burned, my braces had cut up the inside of my lips and my gums were still bleeding. The taste of blood and of the guard's handkerchief in my mouth. He waited to hear my suffocated question before telling me that she was on her way.

—They're calling her now to come get you.

—Where did she go?

I couldn't say her name. The guard looked at me somewhat confused while he held my head with his knees and put his hat back on his skull. His shaved head, like hers. A rough head, covered in menacing bumps.

—I have to tell her. I'm not that man. The one with the sack. He didn't send me.

I'm not going to put her in my sack. I'm not following her, even though I'd like to. I have to find her, to explain to her.

The guard looked at me, puzzled. But I went on explaining.

—She shouldn't call him. I mean, her father.

Days went by and I, not daring to look out the window, abandoned myself to the boredom, morning and afternoon. I dozed with a glass of milk mixed with vanilla and sugar on the table and that sour aftertaste of sedatives crushed to powder in Auntie's mortar. If you had eaten your breakfast you wouldn't be in this condition, she repeated, as if her annoyance was enough to strengthen me. Now you'll sleep like a princess. You'll see. But the realm of my dreams was lined with muddy paths that I walked along, hauling sacks of wet hay.

**When, she asked, breaking glass in my ears, when was I going to stop chasing her with the sack.**

I was recovering, the sacks of hay were getting lighter, and the soggy ground of the paths was drying. But the odor remained. Intense. The pain in my ribs was not fading. I sat in bed copying the notes my classmates sent me every day, without ever coming in to keep me company.

Just a day before I was to get back to school, Auntie allowed me to shower.

—You smell like dirt.

She sang out to me happily from the kitchen where she was making a cake for the guests.

Of wet dirt I thought under the shower. And as I washed my head, my hair newly cut, completely shorn, I heard the knocks at the door. Soft knocks, like steps.

How was I feeling? It was her voice on the other side.

Could she come in? I heard her clearly.

She had brought me a gift.

I got out of the shower and saw that instead of a towel on the hook, there hung a burlap sack. I used it to dry myself in front of the foggy mirror. I put it on when I realized there was a hole for my head and each arm. I jumped with joy and then her knuckles again on the wood. I was ready.

—Your friend is here.

It was the voice of broken glass, and it was she herself who opened the door. We looked at each other carefully. Her hair had grown, her body filled out. She was a girl in uniform, her expression was very sweet now. She told me Auntie had left mint tea for us in the living room.

I let her go ahead and I followed behind her, thinking for the first time of my father, of what my father would say about this girl, and thinking of him I dug a finger between her ribs. I dug it in as if to run it through her. Raising my voice, without even thinking, I began to whisper into her neck again and again the same question:

—Why are you following me?

# Padma Thornlyre
# Mavka #14. Poverty
# Consciousness

it seems I've mastered living one paycheck away
from homelessness, one illness away
from no paycheck in this land where God
is on the money.

but I do have my brother-in-law's
old bachelor chair, its unfamiliar
history of frays, its swivels
and creaks, its broken recliner handle.

I've a boom box with no boom
and *Woodstock* on scratched vinyl,
a futon with a broken frame,
but a good solid cushion to unfold
on my cabin floor beneath a window

open to the stars,
to what's simple and cold,
to what of their faint
light the woods allow in.

two black-tail bucks
sporting velvet
jumped the fence in perfect
unison today after my daughter
tried to shoot them
with my old instamatic. I am drunk

on the fat-leafed mullein,
on how the land turns like a woman where I walk,
on my kid's enthusiasm for the roadside raspberries,
on the white horse grazing
in the Buffalo Creek
meadow just a stone's thrown north.

# Mavka #30. Whiskey

I once had mice in this cabin
and fed them to the god

of ground blizzards.
I now have spiders

but I do not fear them.
One slow, neat shot

of Colorado whiskey.
A day of reading *Mythography,*

how the mind wanders
from Tanya's eyes to an Irish reel

to the long-broken futon frame
I finally busted up three days ago

in a long growl of rage and joy
to a woman I lost in 1984

when my love exceeded
my ability to love

to my beard,
the primal truth of me.

A loud sneeze expelling
all I would let go of, step-

parents, both ex-wives,
the rawhide in which I sweat

old smoke. These
constellations of scars

dimmed by my own minuteness.
I have a sore throat,

a pinched nerve in my shoulder,
but I'm warm for now—

against the vagaries
of wind and its thin draft

seeping through this splintered
window frame, I arm myself

simply, with one more whiskey
and that old yellow blanket.

# Mavka #38.

Indestructible life!—the Sun a yolk that breaks
all morning. A crow shimmers and upon the green

guard-rail bobs as I cross Bear Creek on my drive

to work. I would rather drive into you all that I
mourn: loves gorged by artificial famines—

dogs feeding from graveyards; loves charred
by blood—I would empty

myself of the steak-knives carving up my lover's
wrists, those voices she obeyed, and passions

long ago abandoned to lap-dancing and meth-

amphetamines. Everything that has ever made me
weep distilled into one tablespoon of living brine.

# Mike Valente
# Solitude

Four of us were smashed in the back of the van, absent of any seats or seatbelts. The only seat in the van belonged to the driver, and the other man crouched next to him, facing us during the ride that seemed endless. The floor mats and interior had been stripped as if they were unnecessary, and we sat on the metal-grated floor listening to the instructions from the crouching man, as if he had issued those same commands a thousand other times in his life.

You will be dropped off at a park, he said after an hour of silence had passed. The man was clean-shaven, well groomed, as though his face and jaw had been sculpted with a knife. Outside, the sky was the color of cement. Then he said, You will be expected to observe the children there and report back to us.

The other men in the van were Snowman, Pony Breath, and Jersey. They were attentive like me, yet unsure of how to act or behave once we arrived at the playground. We didn't know if we should ask any questions, and we acted as if we understood everything in full detail.

When the van pulled up next to the curb, the clean-shaven man nodded once, signaling to open the door and begin our mission.

We first waited along the sidewalk next to the small playground, casually like we were waiting to catch a bus. When we discovered a sign that said, *No Adults Without Children Permitted Beyond This Area*, we loitered by the chain link fence surrounding the sandbox, the grass, and the swing set.

Maybe we can grab something to eat, said Jersey. I've been hungry for a while.

It was still early morning, and we anticipated that mothers and babysitters were probably going to bring their toddlers into the playground at any moment.

Let's stay here, said Snowman. We don't want to miss anything.

When the children arrived, they played in the sandbox, ten of them belonging to the same daycare unit, all wearing the same bright yellow shirts, all holding hands, appearing as a line of traffic flares. Initially in the sandbox, some didn't quite know what to do or where to begin, and others immediately scooped up piles of sand, began climbing the jungle gym, riding the steel animals on springs, partial figures shaped like horses, penguins, and sheep.

Pony Breath said that we should flank our positions, spread out so that we didn't seem like four men studying their movements. We distanced ourselves from each other as well as the children in the playground. Jersey walked around a building as if he were taking measurements. Snowman stood on the corner, hinting that perhaps he needed a ride or a taxi. Pony Breath paced back and forth around the baseball diamond of the park as if he were a Little League coach waiting for his team to arrive for practice.

For several minutes, the children seemed like they were having fun, obedient to their guardians. Don't jump from the jungle gym, said one of the daycare attendants. No running by the carousel, said another woman, who was perhaps there with her small daughter. A middle-aged father arrived with his small twins, a girl and boy, and he allowed them to sit in the sand and play with toy trucks and shovels, scooping fervently without adhering to time or place.

From his position on the field, Snowman was fixated on the entire playground, kids throwing a Frisbee, dancing in a hula hoop, not really focused on a single aspect like the sandbox.

We then regrouped, not really sure if we were yielding fruitful results, unsure of how to progress with the mission.

Let's converge on that side, said Pony Breath, realizing that being separated was proving to be useless and ineffective. He had pointed to a soccer game that had commenced on the field opposite the playground, about a hundred meters away. Pony Breath said that our time would be better spent monitoring the children wearing cleats and soccer uniforms.

That's a good idea, said Jersey.

For the first ten minutes of the game, we huddled together on the sideline, the smell of the grass intoxicating and calming. We must have looked like concerned uncles or fathers, blending into the audience, everyone probably thinking that we were the parents of children who weren't theirs.

The parents were intrigued and excited about the action of the game. The teams were equally skilled, lobbing the ball across the field, sprinting nimbly like chaotic chess pieces. Blades of grass flicked off the turf like hot grease on a skillet as the kids ran and pivoted on their cleats.

Jersey asked if maybe we should cheer or yell, feigning interest in the game so that we didn't appear obtuse. Maybe we should act involved, he said, otherwise one of the parents might suspect something.

Pony Breath agreed but wasn't quite sure what we should yell. We don't know any of the names of the kids playing, he said.

We began to clap methodically, but this proved distracting, as we grew more concerned with our rhythm and not the events transpiring on the field.

We still need to pay attention, said Snowman. We can't lose sight of why we're here.

Jersey offered to stand across the street, monitoring the game closely and attentively while the three of us stood and cheered for the children, coordinating our screams and applauses with those of the parents.

Let's stay together for now, said Pony Breath, observing the sky as if it affected our course of action.

We had trouble sustaining our interest in the game, as it was difficult distinguishing the boys from the girls, the uniforms and cleats of equal size and color. All of them seemed to be the same height, wearing headbands, many with short hair.

After the game, we walked for three blocks where the van was waiting for our return. It was parked in front of a Laundromat, and there didn't seem to be anyone inside. Very few cars were on the street, and the van was big and dominant as if the vehicle had staked its claim and belonged there under the dome of the sky.

The clean-shaven man greeted us firmly, looking at each one of us in the eye attentively as we explained to him our progress.

That's adequate, he said. But I may expect more from you.

We drove for what seemed like hours. Our mouths and throats grew parched, having not drank anything over the day, but we didn't ask for water, unsure if they'd be willing to stop. Perhaps there weren't any options, the road unwinding, fields and hills barely disturbed by the thinning sunlight.

We arrived at an industrial building, large and expansive on the outside, and cold and damp in the inside. The clean-shaven man brought us into a corridor with four cots, and we didn't realize how spacious the complex was until we lay down. We didn't remove our clothes, and our shoes still clung to our feet as we reflected on our tasks. Could we have done a better job? Did we miss anything? The four of us seemed to enjoy staring at the ceiling that was very high, probably thrusting itself into the sky in order to make room for its buttressing columns.

The next morning, the clean-shaven man provided a bucket of water and a sponge that we used to bathe ourselves.

Do it quickly, the man said, we don't have much time.

He laid out fresh clothes and shoes for us to wear on our cots. From a distance, they appeared as the same outfits, but upon getting dressed, we realized that they differed slightly. Snowman's shirt had a breast pocket. Jersey's pants had cuffs, and Pony Breath's shoes, while still black like ours, resembled sneakers. We quietly envied the added comfort provided by his shoes, but we didn't say anything.

# We had trouble sustaining our interest in the game, as it was difficult distinguishing the boys from the girls, the uniforms and cleats of equal size and color.

The clean-shaven man fed us a dry breakfast of toast and old pieces of fruit. There was a banana freckled with spots, and we divided it amongst ourselves and closed our eyes as we felt the soft texture of the mush dissolve in our mouths.

There was a thermos of coffee that was still steaming when we poured it into our cups. The coffee was strong, almost gritty like dirt. Everyone thought it to be potent, but we savored the coffee for as long as we could as it streamed down our throats.

Quickly, the man said, standing over us. He always wore boots and clothes with many pockets even though he never carried anything. We must get into the van, he said.

We drove under the blanket of dawn on a long stretch of highway. The sun unearthed from the dark sky like a bright tangerine. Somehow, the inside of the van remained dark, and while the clean-shaven man spoke, we nudged our heads toward the light, anxious to feel the sunlight against our skin.

The man crouched for the duration of the ride, and again, we only saw the back of the driver's head, never glancing into the rearview mirror, solely focused on the windshield and the unspooling road.

You will be dropped off at a mall, said the man, speaking in a sharp cadence as if our day's work were more critical than the last. You will spend time in the food court observing the children eating snacks. You will have the opportunity to watch them in the clothing stores, picking out colorful shirts and tops that they like. If time permits, then you can go into the restaurant that is connected to the department store. As long as there are children with their parents there, you can sit in the restaurant.

The man gave us bills of several denominations, distributing them like a card dealer, steadfast and quick as if he had already counted them and knew their exact amount. Use these to pay for your meal, he said. But you cannot eat the food. Be aware of that. Then, he instructed us to return with more accurate results, not allowing any room for discrepancy or unclarity.

The van unloaded us at the far end of the parking lot, and when we entered the mall, Jersey said that he wanted to stroll around first, stretching out his legs that had been cramped and tight from sitting on the floor of the van.

We'd better sit in the food court, said Snowman. That's where the children will arrive.

Besides, said Pony Breath, we just walked across the parking lot.

We waited for ten minutes in the food court, a group of children spilling into the area of tables, some with parents, others old enough to wander through the mall without supervision.

They slurped on milkshakes, played with dolls that were recently purchased at the toy store by the elevator. Some jumped and twirled in new shoes. Others listened to music. Some children from a large family bounced a new basketball from the sporting goods store.

Jersey remained adamant about strolling through the mall, seeing the bright lights and getting some exercise.

Pony Breath suggested that he sit with us.

What are you going to do by yourself? he said.

Don't worry, said Jersey. I'll keep my eye out for more children.

After he left, Snowman expressed concern about recording the activity of the children in the mall.

Should we use some of that money, he said, to buy pens and notebooks?

I'm not sure if we're allowed to, said Pony Breath. We need the money for the meals in the restaurant.

The mall was filling rapidly, adults with strollers, couples browsing through the many storefronts and vendors selling bracelets.

There's one less of us here, said Snowman. We'll need to be more accurate and precise.

After we watched the children eat ice cream sundaes and waffle cones topped with whipped cream, we made the decision to seek Jersey and continue with our mission. We found him on a bench, staring with a void look on his face, as if there were a brick wall behind his eyes.

We told him that there was enough time to venture into a clothing store before heading to the restaurant, but by the time we reached the shop, there was only one girl with her parents there. They were selecting clothes, probably for the school year. The mother's arm was draped with overalls and a few dresses and the father looked anxiously at his watch before they headed to the register.

We weren't sure if we should remain by the display tables stacked with clothes or meander to the restaurant.

There's a chance that more kids will enter the store with their parents, said Snowman.

But if we stand here too long, said Pony Breath, they might ask us if we need help.

We scouted the area, and we didn't see too many customers lingering in the store. Certainly, the sales associates would have spotted us, asking if we were interested in the merchandise. We thought that we could use some of the money for a pack of socks, or even extra tee shirts, and floated the idea of spending the cash.

Extra garments might come in handy, said Snowman, as if our clothes and rations were not guaranteed, unsure of what we could be wearing the next day.

Jersey remained silent as Pony Breath contemplated our next move.

Let's head over to the restaurant, he said. It's dinnertime, and there certainly will be people and families there.

We ordered our meals from laminated menus, bundles of silverware rolled tightly in napkins at each place setting. A pitcher of ice water was brought to our table, along with a basket of warm bread and butter.

Snowman ordered a hamburger and fries, and Pony Breath ordered a steak with mixed vegetables. Jersey ordered a chicken sandwich and I peered around the restaurant, oblivious to the hot bowl of soup in front of me.

The restaurant filled with families, their young children and toddlers coloring with crayons on placemats, parents asking for high chairs to be placed at the edge of the tables, protruding into the paths of the servers and busboys caring pitchers of iced tea and wet rags.

Snowman stared across the restaurant at the families and children, not really doing much else, as though he were watching a boat sail away.

Some children ate their food heartily, chicken tenders, macaroni and cheese, and square slices of pizza, almost happy to be there, oblivious to everything around them.

The waitress asked us if there was a problem with the food, and for a moment, we weren't sure what to say, worried that we were causing others to notice our behavior.

We're waiting for someone, said Pony Breath.

Let me know if you need anything else, she said, and she left us alone for the duration of the meal.

We allowed the aromas of the food, hot and freshly cooked, to saturate the table. We didn't know when we'd be privy to the smells of delicious food again. We almost wanted to eat every morsel on the plates, devour every portion. We examined the forks and knives in our hands as if they were surgical instruments. We set them down in unison, and then Jersey said that he wanted to take a bite.

I'm not sure that would be a good idea, said Snowman. We're here to observe the children.

He picked up his burger, and Pony Breath reached across the table and grabbed his wrist.

We need to act in accordance with our mission, he said to Jersey. Focus on the mission.

**I think that we've observed enough, said Pony Breath. The more commotion there is, the more difficult it will be to record everything.**

After several minutes of gathering the frenzy in the restaurant—the behavior of the children, their parents trying to maintain control—a new family sat down in the booth next to us, a small girl close enough for Jersey to extend his arm and touch.

I think that we've observed enough, said Pony Breath. The more commotion there is, the more difficult it will be to record everything.

We paid our bill and left the restaurant.

Just before reaching the exit, the waitress asked if we needed containers for our food. Snowman said, No thanks, and she looked at us puzzled, as if a light bulb hadn't been changed.

In the van ride back to the warehouse, we didn't tell the clean-shaven man about Jersey's brief departure in the mall. Over the duration of the ride, we passed fields, some hills with dry slopes that hadn't experienced a rainfall for a while. The dwindling sunlight seemed a thousand miles away.

What did you learn in the restaurant? the man asked.

We explained to him in great detail everything up to that point.

Snowman began reciting the menu items, possible meals that many of the children most likely ordered.

Jersey described the aisles, the manners of the serving staff, and the head count at all of the tables.

What else? asked the clean-shaven man, still crouching, his gaze embedded in the air between us.

Pony Breath described the structure of the mall, the adjacent parking lot, the colors of the signs at every store. He said that children were inclined to enter the stores based on the colors.

We continued driving for several hours, perhaps passing a gas station, maybe a rest stop that didn't seem like it was there the day before. The ride didn't last as long as the previous day, even though it was dark by the time we arrived.

The clean-shaven man brought us into the same lunchroom, placing a tray of cold meat on the table, cooked hours ago and refrigerated in tin foil. After we finished, he showed us to a larger room, the size of a stadium, with four cots in the center.

Snowman stood for a minute observing the great distance and size of the chamber, almost big enough to throw a ball and watch it fall dead before reaching the wall.

None of us said anything, too tired, just eager to fall asleep and get as much rest as possible.

In the morning, upon waking up, Jersey was gone, his cot removed entirely from the room. We weren't even able to recollect where his cot had been, which space on the concrete it had occupied.

There will be one less of you, said the clean-shaven man, toting another bucket of water. It wasn't the same bucket that we used the previous morning, but there was less water, already dirty and murky, and the sponge didn't seem as clean.

Bathe and dress quickly, he said. You will have a very important job today.

We didn't want to inquire about Jersey—Did he decide to leave? Was he asked to leave? We thought that perhaps he was going to rejoin us, maybe receiving treatment for feeling ill.

The clean-shaven man spoke as if he were well-rested, a loud voice that seemed commanding in the morning, direct and focused during the evenings when we were tired and exhausted.

He led us into a section of the complex with a high ceiling again, a concrete floor equal to the length of a runway and not a single window. There was a pile of large, wooden planks on the ground, forming a pyramid. Probably hundreds of them.

You will move these planks from this room to that room, he said, pointing in the distance to another section of the complex. You will receive a tremendous amount of exercise, able to stretch your legs, walk, and increase your stamina, he said. This will benefit you greatly.

He left us for the entire day to complete the task. Initially, the planks didn't seem that heavy, but after the first wave had been completed, we started to feel tired.

Hold the plank over your shoulder, said Snowman. That way, your body can support the weight of it.

Push it along the ground at an angle, said Pony Breath.

We tried all methods, including rotating in shifts of two to carry the planks from one end to the other.

When Pony Breath injured his knee, we took a thirty-minute break, allowing him to recover. Hopefully he'd be able to assist us in completing the job.

Snowman stared beyond the massive wall of planks and into the vast darkness that encapsulated the complex, silent and vexed as if he had forgotten something.

Are you okay? I asked him. Snowman remained idle like a collapsed star. I was worried that he'd lost his concentration, a critical component for completing the job.

I'm fine, he said, gazing as if a menacing light would emerge any second, not wanting to move in case it had.

Every time we reentered that portion of the complex, the chamber seemed different, and it almost became a pleasant experience to reemerge in the darkness of it. That's why I was concerned for Snowman, perhaps not wanting him to feel out of place or distant.

We should be done in another few hours, said Pony Breath, examining his knee as if he were checking a deflated tire. I don't think that it will be too hard.

When we did finish, we evaluated our results—a mountain of planks stacked neatly and quietly, resembling exactly the previous position they had been.

That's when the clean-shaven man thanked us for our work, guiding us into the room with the lunch table where with the same pieces of meat from the previous day were displayed, this time with a thermos of lukewarm tea. The clean-shaven man showed us a book, holding it high above his head like a trophy that we wanted to touch, anxious to place our hands on its surface, a glossy cover that reflected the barbs of light in the room.

I've decided to provide some entertainment for everyone, he said. I will read some passages, and hopefully, you will respond joyfully and amicably.

He opened the book to a preset page and began reading. The passage described a rabbit eating a parcel of food, and then running through a field.

*The rabbit leaped over the hedge,* said the clean-shaven man, reading from the book.

Snowman laughed voluminously and Pony Breath applauded charismatically for the rabbit, saying that he was able to envision the rabbit leaping over the hedge.

The clean-shaven man paused momentarily, examining us as if we were ready for another passage. He looked down at the book and began reading, again the passage about the rabbit, eating, running and jumping.

*The rabbit leaped over the hedge,* said the man, in the same voice, stoic and precise, as if he had read it aloud for the first time.

We laughed and smiled, and the clean-shaven man continued reading, again using the same passage, never turning the page, only looking up occasionally to observe our faces and reactions.

*The rabbit leaped over the hedge,* the man read again. After ten readings, we lost count, and after what seemed like an hour or more, he continued reading, pacing himself so that we could relish the story and prepare ourselves for the next reading. When he finished, he closed the book, nodding his head, signaling that he had come to the end.

I hope you enjoyed it as much as I have, said the clean-shaven man, suggesting that we get plenty of rest, as he was anxious to begin the next day with much excitement and anticipation.

That night, we slept in the same vacuous chamber, our cots neatly prepared as if we were guests at a hostel.

Sleep well, he said. You have a big day tomorrow.


Our breakfast was laid out for us on the same table, a plate of toast, a pitcher of orange juice that didn't taste sweet, and two large bananas that we shared and consumed with much pleasure.

The clean-shaven man stood over us, like a soldier standing at his post, and we wiped our mouths and hands, not wanting to get any food on our clothes that had been neatly supplied for us after we bathed. Pony Breath and Snowman smelled like the water that came from the bucket, and I'm sure that I did, too. But we liked the feel of the clothes, and we thanked the clean-shaven man for his generosity.

You have another task of observing children, said the man. It will involve great diligence and commitment.

He explained our mission in the van, always crouching, always saying everything clearly and emphatically like darts thrown at a bull's-eye. As we passed the hills and the fields that appeared to have been cleansed by the morning light, he said that we were going to a school, and that we had the responsibility of observing the children forming lines, entering the school, and perhaps viewing them through the windows while they performed math problems in workbooks, drawing, and interacting inside the classrooms.

This is going to require great devotion, he said. He leaned forward by a few inches, and for a moment, I watched the thoughts dance in his head. Perhaps he wanted to be at the school himself. Maybe he ardently wanted to accompany us.

The van unloaded us almost a full block away from the school, and we stood on the opposite corner of the school, monitoring the children getting dropped off by a procession of sedans. Some spilled out of a yellow school bus with lunch pails and winter coats that nearly impeded their ability to walk and turnaround. They congregated on a patch of grass, milling around like a flock of ducks. Several teachers lined them up, instructing them to walk into the school, a three-story edifice that spanned the entire block. Behind the building was the basketball gymnasium, and we circled the school, peering into the windows of the classrooms.

When they come out for recess, will they use the empty parking lot as a playground? asked Snowman, pointing to an area that was surrounded by a chain link fence. With the exception of a single utility vehicle, it was vacant of any cars.

The weather is getting chilly, said Pony Breath. They might take advantage of the gymnasium, especially for physical education, wearing only shorts and tee shirts.

The air seemed to calcify like ice in our throats since the early morning van ride, and there were leaves scuttling around in a vortex along the pavement.

Let's make a few circles around the school, said Snowman, before they come out for recess.

We spent the late morning hovering around the block, observing some classes practicing addition and subtraction, the heads of the children barely visible over the elevated edges of the windows. Some teachers were illustrating arts and crafts, positioning an easel at the front of the classroom with various paints and designs. Some children were seated at large tables while modeling clay, inchoate sculptures falling and rising in front of them.

We were getting hungry, but none of us said anything, fully aware that it was

Jersey who wanted to take a bite of his hamburger. Did he eat anything at the mall when he separated from us? Was he even observing any children while walking individually in the shops?

The children spent their lunch time in a large cafeteria, the windows only allowing us to see a few of the tables where the children ate sandwiches, bags of chips, and small cookies that were consumed as quickly as they were removed from their packets.

We were finally confident that we had documented enough information to report to the clean-shaven man, substantial from beginning to end. Snowman didn't even say that he needed a notebook, and Pony Breath was always alert, almost excited at the opportunity to observe the children from all angles and distances. It was by far our best day.

We returned to the spot where the van had dropped us off, the edge of the street that was within shouting distance of a small row of homes.

I don't see the van, said Snowman. All of us scouted the area, craning our necks like we were looking for a body in a crowd.

I don't see it either, said Pony Breath.

We walked up and down the street. Perhaps the van was moments away. I imagined the van swerving around the corner, the sound of the tires crunching gravel and the engine turning like a humming lawn mower.

We spotted a van around the corner, a different color, perhaps even larger than the vehicle that we rode, but we approached it anyway. Maybe we were mistaken about the color and shape of our original van.

This could be it, said Pony Breath, as we increased our pace, only to discover that a mother was unloading her infant from a car seat, returning from running errands, shopping for groceries.

Did we arrive at the street too early? Were we at the wrong location?

Maybe we should return to the school, said Snowman, believing that we obviously hadn't finished our mission, perhaps forgetting a critical task that was necessary before our return.

We stood in front of the school. Several cars lined up, snaking around the corner. A fleet of school buses parked in front, waiting for a signal to move like a convoy of tanks.

We positioned ourselves under a tree. Perhaps the van was going to arrive in the front of the school as well, eager to see us on the job, performing our duties diligently, flawlessly.

The façade of the school was majestic, rectangular windows, names of mathematicians and scholars etched above the large, steel doors. As we looked at the edifice, the long concrete stairs leading to the doors, Pony Breath and Snowman appeared studious, as if they were viewing the horizon past the sea for the very first time.

When the school bell rang, a few cars started their engines. Pony Breath and Snowman might have said something under their breaths, but I couldn't hear them over the cacophony of the clanging school bell broadcasting throughout the city like an alarm.

More cars ignited their engines, like machines in motion at a factory, and Pony Breath and Snowman looked at the school doors, anxious to see what awaited us, nervous to discover the commotion behind the doors.

The children will be coming out, said Snowman, almost weary at what lay ahead.

When the doors flew open, a stream of children gushed down the steps, packed tightly until they reached the bottom, widening like an uncontrollable flow of lava.

Here they come, said Pony Breath, a pebble of fear in his voice.

The chaos felt like a current of energy, the jubilation and screams drowning the engines and cars around us. We watched them as though we were standing on a small bridge. The children ran faster under the open air, toward us, a ferocious wave that was unforgiving, smashing against rocks.

Snowman and Pony Breath stood patiently, as there was nothing we could do but wait for the children.

# Thomas Reiter
# Word Problems

On open-bowling nights we'd see you
after the last frame waiting
to clean the men's room that by then
could have sprouted skunk cabbage.
To our "Looking good, Marty,"
no reply or glance. *Genetic gutter ball,*

one of us would stage-whisper,
breaking ourselves up, your eyes
set wide apart as a 7-10 split.
You were a doodle in our high school margins,
a bear on roller skates, though someone said
you had Japanese shrapnel in your skull.

We couldn't have said why we chose you
or why anyone at all,
but we'd joke, keeping score, that the X
for a strike was your signature. Then
eminent domain took the River Lanes.
The last time I saw you, Marty,

I was doing word problems:
trains starting out toward each other
at the same time from opposite coasts,
and all the variables in between.
Something darkened the page. Centered
in my bedroom window an arm's length

from that homework, you appeared
between me and the sunlight
because my mother had hired you:
peace in Korea, my father was coming home.
I still see myself watching how
you lightly soaped each pane in swirls

like an exercise in the Palmer method,
then angled an inch of squeegee
across the top, the light waiting there,
and brought it down with the rubber blade
in overlapping strokes to return yourself
whole, a man on a ladder doing windows.

At the end you let your gaze pass through
the glass. It seemed you nodded.
I lifted my hand to wave
but you were gone, in your place
the day's bright edges and those trains
and the answers I would need to arrive at.

# Souvenir

*Air from Sunny Southern California,*
that cardboard tube the size of
a toilet paper core says from Uncle Harry's
mantelpiece, and *Close Quickly After Enjoying.*
At the bottom of the label, *Muscle Beach.*

I'm six years old, and Vern Gagne
in American flag trunks has just taken
two out of three falls—a flying
scissors, an unbreakable sleeper hold—
from the hammer and sickle,
though at times the picture faded
and it was like trying to watch
through a dandelion seed head.

My parents and Uncle Harry are playing cards
in the kitchen, and after Friday Night Wrestling
I promised to nap on the couch.
But that *Sunny Southern California*—as I thumbnail
the cap loose it leaps away
to roll under a wing chair and I have to
sweep my arm like a windshield wiper.

I take a deep breath from the tube
through holes punched in the shape of petals.
The *Famous Pacific Breezes* moving
those palm trees on the label? Lost,
and I'm still in that Iowa winter night.

When one day Uncle Harry finds
his souvenir empty, will he remember
the time I was alone in the parlor?
As I wait for sleep, California stands
back in its place, keeping my secret.
Laughter . . . "I'll raise you" . . . "I call."

# The Money Question

As this issue of TLR focuses (however obliquely) on sports, money, success, failure, literature (of course), and money money money, we've been trying to figure out an elegant and nuanced way to ask writers whose work we love, about money and how it fits into the creation of literature. Obviously it's never quite as black and white as "What's more important to you, Mr. Beckett, art or money?" For the modern novelist or poet, there are also matters of success, survival, creature comforts, family, the Foreign Legion, the "industry," the phenomenon of blockbuster art, ebooks, shifting habits and expectations through fractional generations . . . And, well, the economy.

So with all this in mind, we put this question to several writers who we consider in some way essential, and this is how they answered.

**Would you do it for free?**

Yeah. Given the number of hours I work on each book—thousands upon thousands of hours—and the amount I'm paid for each, I feel like I pretty much do write for free, anyway, or close. I also write an awful lot of essays for which I'm paid little or nothing. To me, life is a sand-storm. If you're not building some kind of free-standing hut against the sand-storm, you're as buried as those two people in *The English Patient*. —**David Shields**, author of *Reality Hunger, A Manifesto* and *Body Politic, The Great American Sports Machine*

I already do it for free for the most part, and would certainly continue to do so in many respects. The poetic impulse is not primarily based on making money, which sometimes results in publishers and promoters taking advantage of us. The one thing I seriously balk at is what seems to be a threat to the very idea of copyright. The poet does deserve some recompense, just as the plumber does. There seems to me a move afoot to suggest that literature should be seen as freely accessible to one and all. I'd be for that, maybe, if the same were to apply not only to plumbers but psychiatrists, pig farmers and University presidents. —**Paul Muldoon**, author of *Moy Sand and Gravel* and *The Annals of Chile*

I do it a tiny bit for free now, if it's an interesting enough project (significantobjects .com) or extremely easy (Twitter) or both (this). And when I do it for money, my rate of pay varies by an order of magnitude, which suggests a certain psycho-economic elasticity if not irrationality. One of the reasons I never became a serious blogger was the Samuel Johnson voice in the back of my head ("No man but a blockhead ever wrote, except for money"). But, basically, at this point, yes, I'm a blockhead: writing is how I figure out what I think and feel, and as long as I could publish, I'd still write what I write, even if I weren't being paid for it. —**Kurt Andersen**, author of *Turn of the Century; Heyday* and host of PRI's *Studio 360*

I had to laugh when I read the question *Would I?* I *do* and have done for years. I not only write for no money, I also translate for same and publish books for same. Which, I realize, risks sounding not too bright on my part, particularly when presented as a list. But I'm sure you'll get basically the same response from any poet that you ask; poetry is simply, in itself, not a financially viable endeavor; it doesn't trade on that market. It does, however, trade on other markets, vague ones such as that of recognition and respect and the only-slightly-less vague but thoroughly delightful one of friendship, a network of amity that means that anywhere you go in the world, you can find a poet or poets to connect with perhaps in tacit recognition of our limited numbers and of the fact that only we can pay ourselves, and only with ourselves. There are also concrete, crucial markets on which poetry trades, such as that of employment. For, while I'm not paid to write poetry, I would not have been hired, and thus paid, to teach had I not done that un-paid writing. And as anyone involved in a college or university in the U.S. knows, the incongruity doesn't end with hiring: tenure in the humanities is based not on your work as a teacher, but on your work as a writer, so you're constantly judged on something for which you're not paid and which is, in turn, made more difficult to do because you have to spend so much time doing what you're paid for. It's like having two jobs and two employers; I have a day job working for the state of Iowa as a professor, and I have a real job working for myself and for a concept and potential of culture. And, in fact, I love my day job it keeps me constantly reading both historical and contemporary pieces; it keeps me thinking and learning, and it keeps me in touch with what subsequent generations of poets are doing, which in turn contributes to the other two. This is not to say that I wouldn't *so much* rather be spending my entire year as I spend my summers: writing, translating, publishing books (I have a very small press dedicated to contemporary French work in translation), and working on all sorts of editing and collaborative projects. In fact, the fascinating and fabulous things to do that are guaranteed not to earn you any money seem endless. All that said, I feel incredibly lucky to have the job I have, even if I don't get paid for it. —**Cole Swenson**, author of *Goest* and *Ours: Poems on the Gardens of André Le Nôtre*


Sure, I'd do it for free. I do it all the time for TheRumpus.net. I also visit high school classes and donate books for auction and host fundraisers. I've got no problem doing it for free, if the endeavor is not-for-profit, and seems in the right spirit (i.e. generous, humanistic). It's when someone is going to make money on the endeavor that I get my hackles up. Writing well is hard work and takes time—and that shouldn't be taken for granted. If the endeavor is making money, the writer/s should get their fair take. Pretty basic. —**Steve Almond**, author of *Rock and Roll Will Save Your Life* and *Candyfreak*


Yes, I would, in fact, do it for free—I always figured I'd have to have a second job to pay for the writing job because I couldn't imagine ever making a living as a fiction writer. So, when I do make money for a book, it's kind of amazing to me. And there has always been something a little liberating about being in a field that is not a huge money-making enterprise—there's more room to try things out. —**Aimee Bender**, author of *The Girl in the Flammable Skirt* and *The Particular Sadness of Lemon Cake*

"Money" (reprinted from *Dossier*, No. 2, 2008)

Two drinks down, and there's money
begging to be fucked by me, to fuck me silly,
money's hand clutching at my sleeve—
foolishly aware of how money must rave

all over the city, demanding, begging,
telling lies I need to hear and money
needs to tell. It's ridiculous and sad,
this wanting sharpening money's naked need

as if money were a cock, a cunt that can't stop
coming, and the more it comes the more
it has to come, money money money
making me feel what I can't shut down enough

not to feel in this wanting of not
having I have to have even as I have it.

"Money is a kind of poetry," said Wallace Stevens; "It is intensely sad," wrote Philip Larkin; "It is the anarchy of poverty / delights me," wrote William Carlos Williams, who worked among "The Poor," as he entitled the poem, perhaps without thinking through the cost of that delight.

And in this passage from the Odyssey, it's interesting to see what happens if you substitute "money" for each reference to Proteus, the shape-shifting Old Man of the Sea:

From *The Odyssey*, Book IV, 450-463 (reprinted from American Poetry Review Special Supplement Sept./Oct. 2009)

At noon the Old Man came out of the sea
and found his fat seals and counted them up—
and we were among the first he counted.
. . . Then he too lay down . . .
We rushed him, shouting, and locked him
in our arms, but the Old Man didn't forget
his wily art; he turned into a great, heavy maned lion,
a snake, leopard, a huge boar, then he shimmered
and overflowed and ran like water through
our hands, then fountained up into a tree
with waterfalling branches, but we held on to him,
tightening our grip, holding on desperately.
But when the devious Old Man finally tired,
he spoke to me, asking, Which of the gods
put you up to this, son of Atreus, just what do you want?

—**Tom Sleigh**, author of *Far Side of the Earth: Poems* and *Spacewalk*

I might write for free, but I publish for money. —**Victor LaValle**, author of *The Big Machine* and *The Ecstatic*

I was propositioned by a bond trader of mortgage-backed securities. He told me he could transform me into an MBS trader if I'd give him eighteen months. It was 2004. I loved the notions of making gobs of money. As an artist you don't make gobs of money. And I, like so many people in this crazy money-obsessed culture of ours, adore gorgeous beautiful things. I could easily imagine waltzing through life selecting the finest objects, taking the most exquisite vacations, giving every advantage to my children. What did I do with his offer? I wrote a novel. Because beneath all that desire for the material what I really want is to write. Writing, for me will always win out. Writing for me is the finest object that money can't buy. Not everyone can sit alone at a desk for four years and puzzle through a story. Not everyone gets to or wants to. I want to and I cherish that desire. So as much as I love money and love reading about people who love money—think Scarlet, think Becky Sharpe, Undine Spragg, Lily Bart, Clyde Griffiths, Jasper Milvain from Gissing's *New Grub Street* just to name a few—I love writing and the creative life even more. And in spending so much time on the subject of money, the MBS mess we've made of the American dream of homeownership, the fun we've had with other people's puny debts that represent their everything—I've come to see quite clearly and vividly that with my lovely husband and gorgeous children and my cleaver spirit that takes me far and wide, I see that everything I want I already have. —**Martha McPhee**, author of *Dear Money* and *L'America*

Yes. We all love Samuel Johnson's line, but the truth is most of us do it "for free." We might get some money for a book, but usually when you divide it by the number of years of torment that went into the writing the whole enterprise seems absurd. You have to be seriously stupid to get into this for the money, though the catch is if you are seriously stupid you have the best chance of making a lot of money. I've been paid well at certain times, others not at all. I've always thought of writing and publishing as separate endeavors. They don't intersect that often. I teach full time. That's my job. That's how my family eats, etc. And I'd teach "for free," too, as long as somebody paid me to do it. —**Sam Lipsyte**, author of *The Ask* and *Homeland*

# Ana Maria Spagna Test Ride on the Sunnyland Bus: A Daughter's Civil Rights Journey

*By Ann Beman*

Call me late to the start line, but I've only recently recognized the parental puppetry jogging me around—even as an adult. It's been nine years since my mom died. She was 84. I was 34. You do the math.

I think of her often, and at moments that surprise me—when I smell salt grass on a beach, hear the fabric-rustle of a party dress, taste an egg salad sandwich. And I glimpse a ghost of Mom when my eyes haven't yet hard-focused on my own reflection in a mirror. We had a decent number of years to get to know one another, and I can't blame her for living 60 percent of her life utterly without my existence. My father recently declared that he intends to live to 100, a campaign I fully support. But unless we're talking sports lore or financial tactics, details escape his fuzzy memory. So, for the most part, I script my own stories of the 60 percent of my mother's life I missed, her character, and the various dispositions she may or may not have passed to me. "Ah," I say to myself. "That's why I do like I do."

I still have a lot of questions.

Which is one of the reasons I found myself relating to Ana Maria Spagna's memoir, *Test Ride on the Sunnyland Bus,* in which the author has her own set of questions, and searches for answers about her father, who died when she was a child. She searches, too, for a kinship with the past, and with her future as a lesbian in modern-day America.

Bison Books/University of Nebraska Press, 2010.

For twenty-seven years, '50s civil rights battles were a whisper in Spagna's ear. As part of a lesbian couple living in the woods in a community so remote as to be without phone service, the author has been a non-activist—the opposite of activist. She refers to herself as a coward. "I didn't really believe anything could be done," she writes. "Worse yet, I didn't know *why* I didn't believe."

The questions arise when three seemingly random events collide. First, the world is changing, as it often does, for the worse: "terrorism, environmental degradation, ethnic cleansing, sure, but also closer to home, the seeds of it all, paranoia, xenophobia, plain old-fashioned hate." Second, in a move that reminds me so much of me, it makes my procrastination muscles twitch, Spagna Googles her entomologist brother's research. 'Cause cool bug facts are "fascinating or at least more interesting than what I'm supposed to be doing." But instead of encountering bugs, the author comes across a book about white Southerners in the civil rights movement, and her father is in it. Third, she resumes an activity that inevitably connects her with her father: Running.

I've been on a books-about-running rampage lately, mainly because I too recently rediscovered the sport—as physical exercise, yes, but also as exercise in meditation, transportation, and social connection. Not to mention parental connection. My dad and I both ran in college, as did my mom's dad.

Although it strides a few paces behind family relations and civil rights in Spagna's memoir, running becomes a poignant subplot. As she rediscovers the pleasures of running, the author begins to peek out from her piney wooded home and to break a new trail of whys: "why he acted, why he left [Tallahassee], what happened, in the end."

A seven-month struggle to integrate city buses, the Tallahassee bus boycott started in May 1956, at the same time as the more famous bus boycott triggered by Rosa Parks and led by Martin Luther King Jr. in Montgomery, Alabama. But the movement had begun to wane. Joined by two other white and three African American men, Joseph Spagna—at the time a Florida State University student— stepped up to inject the boycott with new momentum, challenging a Tallahassee ordinance segregating the races on city buses. The plan: To ride the route known as the Sunnyland. "To ride the bus together—three blacks and three whites—to get arrested and to take their case to the U.S. Supreme Court. But it was dangerous as hell."

Lobbing herself back and forth between her remote home in the Pacific Northwest, the Southern California care center in which her mother is dying from cancer, and her Tallahassee research, the author feels pulled between current family emergencies and past tragedies:

> *Always go forward. Never go back.* This had been my father's credo, and he had lived it faithfully from Dartmouth footballer, to Marine Corps deserter, to Florida, to San Francisco, to South America, and to the couch in the family room.
> "'Come on,'" he said once more. "'Run with me.'"
> "'No,'" I said.
> "'Don't tell Mom,'" he said.
> "And he left."

Joe Spagna dropped dead while out running. Eleven years old at the time, the author saw it as an act of betrayal, of desertion. She spent much of her youth pissed off at him: "He'd died too young. He'd abandoned us. For twenty-seven years, I'd been in no mood to forgive my father or even to think much about him. Until, last January, when I headed off to Tallahassee."

The author corresponds with the surviving Sunnyland Bus riders, she attends the fiftieth anniversary celebration of the bus boycott, and immerses herself in 1950s civil rights history. Along the way, she explores her own whys: "I do it because I want to understand the past but also because I desperately want to escape the present," even as she surmises those of her father's cut-short life:

> Maybe running was transcendental like prayer, liberating like a beatnik road trip, only minus the drinks and the chicks and, well, everything, but the wind in your hair, and maybe when you're over forty and the father of three, the wind in your hair is enough. That, and the fat slabbing off like arctic ice, feet slapping like a metronome, and sometimes, every so often, sunlight slicing through the smog and clarity at last!

As a writer, I marvel at Spagna's ability to essay—to root out the precious truffle of meaning in both ordinary and extraordinary settings. One minute she's reading a courtroom transcript; the next, she employs flashback, imagining her father's thoughts within that courtroom scene; and the next minute, she sets down her notebook to go out for a run. Again, running enters the equation, in this case to convey a shift. We shift from then to now, from indoors to out, and from inside her father's head to inside her own. Throughout the book, the author interweaves past and present, research and reflection, monologue and dialogue. The best passages braid her memories of family life before and after her father's passing with the conflict and self-doubt she undergoes on her journey to finally celebrate his role, in her life, as well as in Tallahassee:

It's not about courage anymore. Maybe it never was. It was about grief, common as dirt. For twenty-five years, I'd scripted a story for myself: my dad ran away—from home, from Dartmouth, from Tallahassee, and eventually from us—and then I ran away from Riverside, from the problems of the world, from any place with a telephone. I'd been angry about the former and guilty about the latter for too long when all along I knew the truth: my dad's life, like mine, was pretty much the same as anybody else's. You do hard things. You live the best way you know how. You experience grief, and hopefully, you experience joy. If you're lucky, you share them both.

Spagna's first book, *Now Go Home: Wilderness, Belonging, and the Crosscut Saw*, showcased her prowess with the essay form, tendering a collection as fertile as the woodsy soil in which she works and eventually settles. Seems to me, her trick is to ask herself questions as hard and deliberate as the trail crew labor she performs.

With this new and nuanced memoir, Ana Maria Spagna shows us yet another facet of herself. In the field of universal human questions, "Who am I?" takes a close second to the simple yet elegant, "Why?" The author crosscuts through both in *Test Ride on the Sunnyland Bus*, leaving us with a very hope-in-the-era-of-Obama feeling, as well as a sense that she herself may finally rally a few lobs of activism. My hope-in-the-heyday-of-Spagna is that her next memoir takes us along on that foray. I'll likely read it with my legs draped over the stuffed-chair arms of my favorite family heirloom. "Are you sure you have enough light?" I'll hear my mother say just as I crack open the book.

# Carmine Abate
# The Homecoming Party

*By Marion Wyce*

There's a magnet on my refrigerator that pictures two sweet-faced, pony-tailed girls, perhaps sisters, grinning in a knowing way that suggests they're sharing a private joke. Beneath the image is a caption: *First we get better grades than the boys, then we take their jobs.* My mother gave me the magnet as a stocking stuffer a few years ago, a gag gift that nodded toward the girl I'd been: bookish, ambitious, unwilling to defer to male authority. But according to certain media reports, the sentiment isn't so funny. "The End of Men," a recent article by Hanna Rosin from *The Atlantic*, questions whether we're moving toward a matriarchal society in our post-industrial economy—and whether men will be able to adapt. Rosin notes that U.S. women now earn more college degrees than men and, for the first time, outnumber them in the workforce. Yes, men continue to earn more, but they also lost three-quarters of the jobs eliminated in the recession, with working-class men particularly hard hit. As American women have entered universities and the workforce, they've redefined our understanding of womanhood, Rosin argues, whereas the ideal for men hasn't changed much over time, even as their opportunities have.

Those concerns seem a world away from the small town in southern Italy inhabited by the characters of Carmine Abate's lyrical novel, *The Homecoming Party*. Yet Abate's characters face the same fundamental struggle: How to be a man when the rules of the game have changed. Abate has published widely over the last twenty-five years—novels, poetry, essays—but he's a relative newcomer to U.S. readers; this

Translated by Antony Shugaar; Europa Editions, New York, 2010.

novel, which received several notable Italian awards, is just his second to be translated into English. He structures his book around one of the town's favorite traditions, a Christmas Eve bonfire. Twelve-year-old Marco and his father, Tullio, sit beside the fire trading stories, an archetypal ritual of manhood. Tullio has a fatherly purpose for this conversation; he wants to *release* his regrets, as Marco tells us:

> Sparks moved through the air all around us, like swarms of crackling bees; they fell silent as their inner flames burnt out, and they dropped on our hair and clothing like a blizzard, and my father said there'd never been such a fire, a perfect bonfire to toss all our worst memories into, he said, and set fire to them in a flash, and for all time.

The novel is concerned with how the past both molds and haunts us, and evocative images like this one appear throughout the book, giving it the dreamlike, visual feeling of memory. As Tullio shares his memories and secrets and Marco recalls his own, the story moves around in time, always returning to the ritual of the bonfire. Through what they reveal to each other—and what remains unspoken—father and son create a shared narrative about how tradition binds them, both to each other and to expectations about what it means to be a man.

It's fitting that most of the novel's action occurs in the past, because Marco's and Tullio's relationship exists more in memory than in the moment. In post-war Hora, the ethnic Albanian enclave where Marco's family lives, men are still the providers for their families, and women still the caretakers. We get a sense of Hora's rich culture through the descriptions of holiday rituals and food and the Arbëresh phrases that Abate weaves into his prose and that Antony Shugaar has elegantly preserved in this translation. But the idyllic rhythms of life in Hora are under assault because there's little work to be had. So men like Tullio seek work abroad (France, in his case) and return home only for extended visits around the holidays. The hopeless circumstances that force many southern Italians into the emigrant life are an abiding theme across Abate's body of work. A native of Calabria, the southern Italian region where this novel and many of his other works are set, Abate himself immigrated to Germany at a young age before eventually settling in northern Italy.

Through the innocent and honest voice of Marco, Abate makes plain the wrenching effect that emigration has on the families left behind. Marco idolizes Tullio and struggles with his long absences; it doesn't matter to him if his father is making sacrifices for the family's future. "The future, for a child, is an empty word. I wanted to be close to my father every day of my present life. Always." Marco's sadness pains Tullio, who wants his son to understand the sense of desperation he often felt: "Try and imagine that an unscrupulous man, a born whoremonger, points a pistol at your head and says to you: 'Leave, or I'll pull the trigger!' What would you do?"

The story alternates between Tullio's and Marco's perspectives as we piece together their history and the painful memories that Tullio wants to burn in the fire. He shares secrets with Marco: Tullio was married once before, and his older daughter, college-aged Elisa, is the child of his first wife, not Marco's mother. He has gotten into a bloody fight with Elisa's married lover and would have killed the man if he had the chance. But these actions are not what Tullio regrets. It's what he didn't do that torments him. Fulfilling his primary duty as a father—earning money to support his family—means abdicating others: being a constant presence in his children's lives, teaching Marco how to be a man, protecting Elisa from harm. "I thought I knew you well, and instead I didn't know anyone, not even myself, if I think about it carefully," Tullio says.

While Tullio unburdens himself of his secrets, we gradually realize that Marco still holds onto his own. Marco recounts vivid stories from his childhood, about playing in the ravine with his dog, chasing after his soccer ball, hunting with his father during holiday visits, surviving a life-threatening illness. But these memories are just pictures in his head; he doesn't share all these details with his father.

> Here we go, I thought: maybe my father wanted to draw me out, because he lit another cigarette and said nothing for a very long time [. . . .] I talked to fill the silence with the words that my father wouldn't let me forget. I spoke in bursts, my eyes glazed over, as if I was watching myself in a badly edited movie.

As their conversation continues, he contemplates telling his father a dark secret: that he shot Elisa's lover, who was attacking her. "In my mind, I struggled to find the right words: I had to do it, pa, or he would have killed her . . . ." And above all, Marco doesn't tell his father the truth that would break his heart: he, too, plans to leave Hora to work as an emigrant.

As a coming of age story, *The Homecoming Party* is by turns fatalistic and touching. Marco isn't choosing his future so much as becoming a man by repeating his father's choices. In the novel's final chapter, Tullio reveals his big surprise: he's staying in Hora, for good. To mark the end of his emigrant life, he tosses into the bonfire the suitcase he took on his travels. He thinks maybe he'll start a cinder block factory, and Marco can work there one day, too, so he won't need to leave home. Marco keeps to himself what he's already decided: "I knew what awaited me one day, and after all, I wasn't that worried about it. One day, I would buy a faux-leather suitcase. When I was eighteen years and seven months of age, to be exact." Thus Marco's education is complete. As a boy, he wanted to be just like his father—and he will be, even if it means suffering in just the same ways his father did. Elisa is the character who displays a sense of agency about the future, studying at university, moving to Paris because that's what she *wants*. For Marco, desire seems beside the point, almost inconceivable. He describes how, years later, he used his father's old gesture to explain why he too needed to leave: "I held my fist up to my forehead, as if I was holding a gun, and waited for him to speak." The image is bleak, to be sure, but it's also Marco's tribute to his father. What Abate seems to want from us as readers is not to judge Marco's decision but simply to understand it. True, there's danger in allowing our futures to be constrained by tradition and example, but Abate's moving novel reminds us there's love in it too.

# Paul Guest
# One More Theory about Happiness: A Memoir

# Alex Lemon
# Happy: A Memoir

*By Renée Ashley*

Really? Prose by poets? Certainly. But poets and happiness? It's an improbable coupling under any circumstances let alone with the staggering somatic blows—Paul Guest's near total paralysis and Alex Lemon's series of strokes and seizures—that are chronicled in these memoirs. Yet, a poet's penchant for precision leaves words like *happy* and *happiness* begging—each bordering on meaninglessness until the poet tips it over, examines its undersides, and tells us what he finds there. Both Guest and Lemon are exceptional, though contrastive, examiners and articulators. They're not new to recording their stories. They're celebrated poets, both young and male with multiple books and awards already behind them; they're intuitive and they're smart. They know how to happify a book and a snag reader with the hook of irony.

The poet Jane Kenyon, who suffered from severe depression and died of leukemia in 1995 at the age of forty-seven, set out what I am certain is the fundamental nature of happiness in a poem called exactly that: "Happiness." It's written head-on, but in a poet's head-on manner, by tropes and achingly precise images masquerading as examples that wring nuanced emotions into the heart of the reader. It's an excellent lens through which to view both memoirs. Her poem begins like this:

> There's just no accounting for happiness,
> or the way it turns up like a prodigal
> who comes back to the dust at your feet
> having squandered a fortune far away.

*One More Theory about Happiness*, Ecco/HarperCollins, New York, 2010. *Happy: A Memoir*, Scribner/ Simon & Schuster, New York, 2010.

Happiness *turns up*. Happiness is the prodigal, not you. And it turns up in spite of everything, in spite of a body's infelicities. I have not read much quite as *true* as this poem. To my mind, pure-and-lasting happiness is a hyper-fictional telos, and it's plenty clear that illuminated moments of *impure* happiness are far more interesting—and more credible. And credibility in memoir, as we all know since the media crap-storm that stemmed from the Frey novel-cum-memoir, *A Million Little Pieces,* is not an insignificant consideration. Life rarely, if ever, takes the shape of art, but memoir is elastic and adaptable. It's a forgiving form, and when such an abbreviated, selective story is constellated around a single life-altering reversal, a sense of this-then-that—of causation and consequence, as well as, one would think, culpability—is not only feasible but anticipated.

Guest's *One More Theory about Happiness* is essentially his straightforward retelling of the accident in which, at twelve, he broke the third and fourth vertebrae of his neck, along with both arms, and was permanently paralyzed. The facts are carefully articulated—a bike that's old, too large, in shabby condition, loaned by a well-meaning teacher, and, it turns out, brakeless; the out-of-control ride down the steep incline of the teacher's yard; the collision with the hidden drainage ditch that throws him "over the handlebars, catapulted, tossed like a human lawn dart into the earth"; the well-meaning man next door who literally picks the young Guest up from the ground and attempts to set him on his feet, urging him "to shake it off, to get over the scare, to stand" on his own; and Guest's beautifully and briefly drawn collapse: "My head fell over," he says, "like a flower on a broken stem. My cheek rested against my chest grotesquely. Without saying another word they softly laid me on the grass again."

The details of Guest's limited recovery (he remains in a wheelchair and writes with a mouth stick) are presented vividly yet unsensationally—the torturous collar meant to immobilize his neck ("made of two stiff halves, each wrapped in a bandage-like sleeve . . . . Beneath the chin was a hard shelf . . . . When snapped together, both pieces held the neck and head still. They also held in the body's heat . . . ."), and the four long bolts screwed into his skull that stabilized his head within the halo. Whether by nature or design or both, Guest has chosen to tell his story in true Wordsworthian style; what must have been an overflow of powerful emotion now recollected in tranquility. He sticks with the past tense to keep it that way. But there's an unspoken truth, one I feel most strongly, in *One More Theory About Happiness*: it's restraint, the considerable effort Paul Guest must have made to make his heartbreaking story a sort of personal, literary Switzerland. It's admirable on a human level—and frustrating on a reader's level. Though he does let the reader inside, to revelations that skip easily over sentiment to startle: "Great grief filled me up," he tells us, "I seemed to breathe it, but what freed me what this: if my arms never worked again, never dressed myself, or combed my hair, if I depended on others to do these things for the rest of my life, I no longer had to be, or even could be, who I once was. What I once was. I was broken. And new." *New*? That's a shocking and incredible perception for a recently paralyzed young boy. How could this be? Where are the horn-blasts of his anger? of his frustration? We see bits, tiny glimpses of these, but wouldn't these emotions have pushed hard to make their way to the forefront of this story? Perhaps Guest did not want to relive those feelings, though he had to have done so in writing the book. More likely, he thought his emotions weren't the point; so, perhaps he gave us a taste and figured we would extrapolate the rest. But, undeniably, I have internalized his calmly written account so deeply that I've become hysterical *for* him, and I'm projecting—how can this have happened to a child? It's so unfair! Of course, we do see him struggle, both physically and psychologically—the path to adaptation is littered with painful and disappointing setbacks. And you can't help but fall in love with the young man who wrote this book, with its wry title and what, in my own mind, must be its quelling of raw, unbowdlerized grief and anger in addition to his physical pain. But he apparently really is the good boy our mothers told us to keep a lookout for. He doesn't make waves, at least not in this memoir. His choices are considered and deployed. His style tells me: *It's done now. This is the story.* He does not assign blame. (There's no mention, however, of whether his parents were as generous.) And I can't help but wonder how much of the knowledge and maturity he attributes to his young self is a product of a writer's confluence of memory with the gifts of adulthood. And it may not matter in the end. Guest's good heart and sense of humor—along with his impressive writing—deliver the story as he wanted his reader, finally, to know it. And it's a good, horrible story. And in the end he finds poetry—and his is fabulous poetry, funny, full of thought, and intense—and he finds love. He's become the young man we hope moves in next door, and he has given us this surprising and big-hearted book through which we can get to know him.

And then, of course, there's the boy our mothers told us to stay away from. The one who not only makes waves, but is, himself, a sea full of roiling whitecaps and undertow, of unharnessed energies and misdirection. It is no surprise that Alex Lemon chose a hyper, present-tense novelistic approach for his memoir, *Happy*. His life had been one of extremes even before his first stroke; what other mode could have captured the desperation of such a bitter and manic story of self-destruction and genuine psychological and physical pain?

The portrait he draws of himself is electrifying and horrifying and brilliant. Lemon, known to his college friends as Happy, is the freshman power-partier, baseball jock, busy womanizer, full-time boozer and salad-bar-selection-of-drugs partaker, and is so used to being wasted that when he suffers his first bleed from a vascular malformation in his brain stem he seems uncertain whether it's really serious or just a particularly fucked-up day in Lemonland. Between frenzied bouts of substance abuse, he makes his way, finally, to the MRI that spells out the extent of the devastation deep in his brain stem. His disbelief, his anger and horror, are made visceral for the reader. Shortly, his denial will be as well. He becomes an exaggeration of what he had been—drinking even more, taking even more drugs. And in a way it seems right, at least true to character: out of the blue his own brain turns on this young-man-on-the-move, party-pounder, team player, and he reacts by intensifying his established pattern of abuses, behaviors laced now with a serious dose of dark introspection when he can swing it. Later he says, "I started drinking on the bus after my neurology checkup . . . . Now I'm pounding gin and whiskey and beers before games. Smoking joints in the port-a-potty. Popping pills. I don't want to be alone but I can't stand the people around me so I stay as fucked up as I can . . . Saturday, I ate shrooms, and sipped rum in my room . . . ." He continues to play ball, convinces himself he's getting better, lies to the doctors, lies to his coach and his friends, to his mother, but he's obsessed with his condition. He starts reliving the childhood sexual abuse he suffered from the hands of an older male cousin. His fears amp up, along with his anger and resentment. He suffers another bleed. He knows he's losing himself and makes the choice to undergo an extraordinarily risky brain stem surgery to stop the bleeding. His eccentric, itinerant sculptor-and-art-teacher mother is the only stabilizing force he knows and can finally talk to—and she sticks with him through his racking surgical convalescence—until, still severely compromised, he pushes her out of his recuperative nest, and takes up, one more time, his self-destructive lifestyle. I found myself asking why I, why any reader, shouldn't just give up on him. He was a terrible mess, was doing nothing to help himself, and it was making me crazy. And then I realized that, as an older, and female, reader, my own lifelong-empty tank of oxytocin, the mothering hormone, and a similarly unburdened vessel of mothering instinct in general, had suddenly been filled and the juices had kicked in. I wanted to find him and smack him upside his poor damaged head and say, "Knock it off, Asshole!" and then protect him from the unfairnesses of a broken body and from himself. But—and this is the critical issue—I did not put the book down. Between the spellbinding prose and the vitality and stinging surprise of his ability to keep going, I was hooked. Lemon is a phenom; he's electric, he's dangerous, and in danger. He's extreme. And extremely talented.

In a brief epilogue, Lemon tells us he is teaching, writing, trying, still against great odds, to carry on. "There are days I can't read," he says, "days my face, my body go numb, and a couple of times each year I rush to the nearest hospital for an MRI and a new battery of tests. But after a decade of living with a black hole inside me, three years ago, I tossed out all my drugs and booze. I . . . learned to live without doing anything at all." I was shocked. It was a confession that blindsided me. Not the *booze,* but the *love.* I was relieved. And then released.

I had a friend who used to tell me, "If you want *fair,* you have to go to another booth." I tend to forget everything, but I've never forgotten that. What has happened to Paul Guest and to Alex Lemon isn't fair. But it's likely that *fairness* and *happiness* are kissing cousins. Perhaps both are things glimpsed and registered and the memory is what keeps us going on, waiting for the next, unexpected flash of the same. Kenyon says:

> happiness is the uncle you never
> knew about, who flies a single-engine plane
> onto the grassy landing strip, hitchhikes
> into town, and inquires at every door
> until he finds you asleep midafternoon
> as you so often are during the unmerciful
> hours of your despair.

Guest and Lemon have enacted their stories and despairs in character. They appear to have written their lives, both vastly different and shudderingly alike, as they believe they have lived them so far. What could be more apt in delivering the truth of character and the facts of a life to a reader? And what more sobering than such damn sad stories with their nearly happy endings?

# Bei Dao
# The Rose of Time: New and Selected Poems

*By Andrew McKay*

Bei Dao is not a poet who backs away from taking a stand. In *The Rose of Time, New and Selected Poems*, the poem, "Huida" ("The Answer"), written during the 1976 Tiananmen Square demonstrations, providing a rallying cry for the pro-democracy movement and Tiananmen protests of 1989, calls out:

> Let me tell you, world,
> I—do—not—believe!
> If a thousand challengers lie beneath your feet,
> Count me as number thousand and one.

Within this landscape of political oppression, Bei articulates grave concern over the abuse of language. In "The Morning Story," language is turned against itself to control and distort reality, to create fear among the populace:

> A word has abolished another word
> a book has issued orders/to burn another book
> a morning established by the violence of language
> has changed the morning.

An untitled poem in this collection ends ominously: "The exile of words has begun."

Bei's range of expression also includes a wonderful sense of playfulness. In "On Eternity" about a couple sharing dinner in the afterworld he writes: "Chatting heart-to-heart with sheep / we share a lovely wine / and under-the-table crime." In

---

Edited by Eliot Weinberger; New Directions, New York, 2010.

"Awakening" a sense of warmth emanates from "There are times sunlight still holds / the exhilaration of two dogs meeting."

Yet, in Bei's poetry, exuberance can take a defiant tone. In "Let's Go," Bei compels us to break free of our boundaries through the liberation of movement and experience the world beyond our immediate surroundings: "Let's go— / the road, the road / Is covered with a drift of scarlet poppies."

Out-of-country during the 1989 uprising, Bei was barred from reentering China and has been living in exile ever since. With this in mind, the sense of urgency that fills Bei's poetry has immediate context. I find the most moving poems to be those in which Bei dramatizes the pain of being an outsider. In "Old Places," we feel the frustration of someone who can only return to his homeland in his mind:

> At the window just now
> I saw a sunset from my youth
> visiting old places again
> I'm anxious to tell the truth
> but before the skies go dark
> what more can be said.

Similarly, in "A Picture," we feel the pain of separation from his daughter:

> your name has two windows
> one opens toward a sun with no clock-hands
> the other opens toward your father
> who has become a hedgehog in exile.

# Alejandro Zambra
# The Private Lives of Trees

*By Ruth Curry*

In my experience, nothing good happens between the hours of three and five in the morning. The best case-scenario involves an umpteenth examination of the bookshelves, a trepiditious glance out the curtained windows—is that the sun?—a survey of the pharmaceutical collection, and then perhaps a period of tossing and turning: Does my boss hate me? How about my best friend? What did she really mean by that joke? Where is X; why aren't they home yet? And at their worst, these are the hours reserved for ill-advised phone calls, unnecessary drinks, emails best left unsent. When Colette writes in *The Pure and the Impure* of the abyss at five, suffered by devotees of the senses at five sharp every evening, it's tempting to think she was referring to the five o'clock morning hour, the hour in which the peaceful luxuriate in well-earned REM cycles and the uneasy see the encroaching rays of the sun and wonder what they did to deserve this sleepless night. These are also prime storytelling hours, kicked off, much earlier, with innocent bedtime stories, that then move into the danger zone—the unconscious narrative of dreams or the sleepless reconstructing of memories, imagining conversations, or speculating about the future.

    *The Private Lives of Trees*, Alejandro Zambra's second novel, begins also with a bedtime story: the story of two trees, a baobob and a poplar, and what they talk about at night while humans are asleep. Julián, the protagonist, tells the story (which is also called "The Private Lives of Trees") to his stepdaughter Daniela while waiting for Daniela's mother, Verónica, to come home from a drawing class. Julián is a profes-

Translated by Megan McDowell; Open Letter, Rochester, NY, 2010.

sor six days out of the week, and on the seventh, he writes—"he puts off his literary ambitions until Sunday, the way other men devote their Sundays to gardening or carpentry or alcoholism." Recently he finished a very short book (forty-seven pages) about tending bonsai. *The Private Lives of Trees* (the book, not the bedtime story) is also very short (ninety-four pages), preceded by another book, *Bonsai*, Zambra's first. There's more than a coincidental resemblance, it seems, between Julián and Zambra, his creator. This is only one of many indications that *The Private Lives of Trees* is not really about trees at all, but rather about stories and authorship and how we use them to structure our experiences.

Back in Julián's world, the night's installment of "The Private Lives of Trees" ends, though Verónica still hasn't returned from her drawing class. "When she returns, the novel will end. But as long as she is not back, the book will continue. The book continues until she returns, or until Julián is sure that she won't return," the narrator, who is not quite Julián, tells us. Writing that refers to itself as writing begs numerous questions—is this really a novel, is that what we're being asked to believe? A book, sure—it has pages, and a cover—but a *novel*, with made-up characters and a imagined story . . . ? But Zambra's sure hand leads us through these metafictional switchbacks more or less intact. While Julián waits for Verónica, the stories continue; not about trees any longer, but in the form of the aforementioned early morning hours of nervous self-soothing behaviors that get us through sleepless and painful nights. Julián remembers his childhood (notably rife with books and other references to fiction), his mother's singing, his previous girlfriend Karla—"His memories of Karla were almost exclusively tied to the memories of the books that he hadn't brought with him . . . Now Karla is nothing more than a book thief. That's what he calls her sometimes, between clenched teeth, while looking vainly over the bookshelves: book thief."—and when he exhausts his stories from the past, he imagines what Verónica is doing, with what men, and how many times, before he turns to the future, to what Daniela as an adult will think of his book, what her boyfriend will be like. All of this, Zambra leads us to understand, is to keep the novel going: "The novel continues, if only to comply with an unfair decree: Verónica has not returned."

With the movement of Julián's fixation from Verónica to the grown-up Daniela, we begin to see where Zambra is taking us. Julián, tortured in the here-and-now, chain smoking and drinking tea while waiting for Verónica, "wants to catch sight of a future that can exist without the present . . . the future is Daniela's story." Daniela, all grown up in his imagination, is a psychologist who has read his second book, not the bonsai book but its successor, "a love story, nothing unusual: two people construct, freely, deliberately, and guilelessly, a parallel world that naturally, quickly, collapses." This, again, for what it's worth, is a neat summary of Julián's relationship with Verónica, which we have just relived via Julián's 3 AM recollections.

The adult Daniela, however, is not perhaps Julián's ideal reader. "Why is it necessary to salvage stories, as if they did not exist for themselves?" she wonders. Stories do exist for themselves; they are there, moving peacefully and unobtrusively beneath the currents of our daily experience. While Zambra seems to be saying that there is something useful, even redemptive, in making the effort to haul them up from below the surface. Indeed, at times, storytelling is all we can do, its narrative order the only comfort we can give ourselves. Even this, though, is not what Julián or Zambra seems to settle for.

"It would be better to close the book, close the books, and to face, all at once, not life, which is very big, but the fragile armor of the present," Julián thinks, well into the night of Verónica's not-return. And indeed, this is finally what he does, walking Daniela to school, avoiding the puddles the rain has left, kissing her goodbye, letting her go, but only, as Daniela says, for now.

# Neil LaBute
# Filthy Talk for Troubled Times:
# And Other Plays

*By Jody Handerson*

Right around the time Neil LaBute was studying theater at Brigham Young University in Provo, Utah, I was completing my own undergraduate degree in theater at the University of Utah, some forty-five miles away. One might say that we are both products of a similar generation and milieu. We are, here in the West, a community of plain talkers. This is not to say that we are rude, but perhaps given to a bit of bluntness now and then. So, in reading LaBute's collection of seven short plays *Filthy Talk for Troubled Times: And Other Plays,* I looked forward to, at the very least, some cultural resonance, and more optimistically, to the work of a possible kindred spirit.

LaBute's career includes film (*In the Company of Men*, his acclaimed and hackle-raising debut), a short story collection, and a number of plays, which have been received in the theater world with the same withering accolades as his screen work. LaBute doggedly pushes and expands interior experience and boundaries. His first produced play and this collection's title piece, *filthy talk for troubled times*, starts off with an emotionally exposed, sometimes wry and often bittersweet (or perhaps just bitter?) look at relationships, or lack thereof, between men and women. Chronologically, he moved on then to the thorny subject of racisim in *the new testament*, and then an ultraviolent take on violence in children's sports in *i love this game*. From there, LaBute returns to relationships with romance and the furies where he continues to explore the idea of personal and sexual power—with the added twist of non gender-specific characters. The series finishes with two short pieces: a mono-

Soft Skull Press, New York, 2010.

logue titled *the war on terror*, which is a rather raw take on post-9/11 perceptions of Middle Eastern culture, and *helter skelter*, an argument between a pregnant woman and her errant spouse with a truly Mansonesque ending.

"Life is funny and beautiful and weird and I'm here to try to capture some of that on paper," LaBute states in the preface for the collection. In *Filthy Talk for Troubled Times* (you have to love that title) we get a flat-out poke in the face of sexuality, sexism, misogyny, and feminism. LaBute alternates between groups of characters, men and women, with no real interaction between genders—a statement in and of itself. The characters are base examples, almost caricatures; the insensitive, shallow, homophobic male and the strident, eternally dissatisfied female.

> **WAITRESS 1** Actually, the last thing I want is to be alone, but . . . the other last thing is to be with someone.

Is it funny? Well—yes, in that things-I've-often-wanted-to-say-but-didn't sort of way. It reminds me of a particularly spicy version of an early Greek play (think Aristophanes, *Lysistrata)*, even sporting few long sections of monologue à la Greek chorus tossed into the mix. Men and women, needing each other, but in profoundly different ways, peripherally aware that something is not working but unable and/or unwilling to make the sort of compromise that would bring them closer together.

> **MAN 3** . . . fuck, I'm glad I'm a guy! You know?
> **MAN 5** Yeah, why's that?
> **MAN 3** . . . because then I don't have to date 'em. [guys]

As you might have guessed, LaBute's work is not for the prudish reader. His characters hold forth in language so consistently ripe, that my reader's ear was rock-concert-numb after the first few pages. I was reminded of a recent conversation I had with my newly single and avidly dating, 78-year-old father, who had just seen his first R-rated movie in several years: "We would have enjoyed it more if there wasn't so much dirty language," he said, in a what's-the-world-coming-to tone (*Up in the Air*—George Clooney, talking dirty . . . oh my!). Which begs the question, setting certain possibly prim notions aside, does the use of profanity add anything or are we simply drawn in by something so overtly on the edge of propriety? If you lift away the naughty language, does the author have anything interesting to say?

From my perspective, it's an unequivocal yes. LaBute uses profanity like a scalpel, carving away layers of propriety to expose the raw, oft-unsightly, emotion beneath the character's actions and thoughts. Ripe language becomes the common denominator, the cathartic vehicle, the them-us link. Which works (unless you are one of those people who can sit blissfully in rush-hour traffic, late for an appointment, and placidly forgiving the asshole who just cut you off) because though these issues are charged with the emotion of the everyday, they are undeniably controversial and universally topical. We all know, first hand, that men and women have different perspectives on sex and relationships—nothing new there, but LaBute uses "language" to push the point home with painful accuracy.

*The New Testament*, LaBute's second work in the collection, is an unsettlingly funny commentary on racism, set in a familiar café venue. The author suggests that the character of the actor appear in "yellowface" for "effect." Then he rolls out a single scene with three characters: a writer and producer meeting an actor for the first time and wrangling though a racist theme: you're not right for the role of Jesus because you are Asian and we didn't know it.

LaBute uses an excruciatingly familiar diatribe to move the scene forward: The writer and producer share an "Asian" coconut dessert along with an uncomfortable helping of xenophobic commentary.

> **WRITER** Hey, you're the one doing it! I'm just pointing it out. (takes another bite.) This stuff really is magnificent. (To ACTOR.) I can't believe you're from over there—the Far East or wherever—and you don't like coconut. (Beat.) That's weird.
>
> **ACTOR** I live in Seattle. (*the new testament*)

Once again the characters have a stock feel, especially the excruciatingly predictable bigotry of the writer and producer. LaBute doesn't dance around the boundaries of propriety, he steps boldly across and thumbs his literary nose at us from the other side. Is it offensive? You bet. Subtlety and LaBute are not good buddies. Yet, we are allowed some comfort in that these characters maintain an almost cartoonlike quality. Had he chosen to elevate the tone of the piece, excise the overt stereotypes and add dimension and complexity to the characters, I think it would be easier to shrug the piece off, relegate it to just another liberal commentary on moral shortcomings. It wouldn't be funny if we didn't all know somebody like that—but, it also wouldn't be as moving if we hadn't ourselves explored the edge of stereotypes and clandestine bigotry.

The rest of the collection moves on through sports violence, guilt and recrimination in a same-sex couple breakup, a meaty eight-page monologue on terrorism and a final shot at infidelity with a rather graphic on-stage suicide. Throughout LaBute's work we revisit that overwhelming sense of disconnect, a realization of the gulf between needs and desires, men and women, intention and reality—yet in the midst of all this he manages to capture that half-funny, half-sad nugget of authenticity, the oops, been there, done that, said that, or had that feeling. And for me, that's the hook: that LaBute is able to use the humor and stereotypes as a way of bringing the work closer to the bone, allowing the occasional rare peek at inner redemption.

> MAN 5 But then I think, "what good would that do?" So I don't. But I suffer because of it. Seriously . . . Things I say, guys I fuck over at work, the drop of a hat, or women. *All* those women. I reflect now and then about that stuff. Question it or study myself in the mirror, I'm always looking, asking, "Who am I? Am I this very shit that I imagine myself to be?" (*filthy talk for troubled times*)

I see two ways of looking at the work, as revelatory of our own innate flaws or through the assumption of safety in moral superiority. (Either way, it resonates.) The very best of Western plain-speak, a bold an uncompromising delivery: Here it is, or rather here *you* are—now deal with it.

# The Shortlist

### Javiar Marias
**Bad Nature, or With Elvis in Mexico**
*Translated by Esther Allen; New Directions, New York, 2010*
I don't care about Elvis, I can take him or leave him; but if hanging out with Elvis means hanging out with the narrator of Javiar Marias's novella, I'm in. Elvis really did make a movie, ridiculously titled *Fun in Acapulco,* and the official story is that he used a stunt double to film the parts actually shot in Mexico. But while I know that those events are simply the jumping off point for a story that is from then on made up, I still have to say "official story." Because even though Ruibérriz de Torres is a fictional character, the story *feels* so real, so true, that I believe it. I believe that Ruibérriz went with the film crew to Mexico as Elvis's translator. I believe that what happened there was so horrible, of course Elvis would deny being in Mexico—ever. This rambling, babbling, circuitous man, Ruibérriz de Torres, does not stop his brain for one minute of this story, and I love that. —*Jena Salon*

### Paul Kilgore
**Losing Camille**
*Black Lawrence Press, Brooklyn, NY, 2010*
Paul Kilgore's *Losing Camille* attempts to find that which is distinctly American. Passing through a medley of mid-American families, Kilgore takes us to places that

are familiar by turns, and antic at others. Looking closely at ourselves is never particularly pleasant, but *Losing Camille* is a portrait of small-town people drawn the
way Twain and O'Connor drew them: They are funny, they are stubborn, and they
certainly show their teeth. Kilgore's first story collection is a fine example of light
focused: We are flawed, but at least we know it. —*J.D. Reid*


# Steven Moore
## The Novel: An Alternative History: Beginnings to 1600
*Continuum, New York, 2010*

*The Novel: An Alternate History*, by Steven Moore, is a vigorous, indispensable
rebuttal against long-held Anglo-centric beliefs that the novel originated in the
eighteenth century. Its disregard for other pieties (realism, religion, and Dale Peck),
and its breezy style, keep it entertaining without being academic. In seven hundred
pages, extending from 1990 BCE up to Cervantes, Moore's familiarity with translated
works and scholarly criticism proves that, though they don't resemble something by
Dickens or Balzac, ancient Egyptian and Greek works (among others) are indeed
novels, and bear great likeness to much current fiction. His Introduction alone is
essential reading. —*Jeff Bursey*


# Linda Lê
## The Three Fates
*Translated by Mark Polizzotti; New Directions, New York, 2010*

To Americans, Vietnam conjures napalm, protest and counterculture. French author
Linda Lê will let us remain ignorant no more. In poetic and dizzyingly mad prose,
we see the Vietnamese families who were torn asunder after the fall of Saigon. The
Three Fates is the story of three Vietnamese "princesses," living in France who plot
to reunite with the father they left behind. Inspired by King Lear, Lê depicts an
unjust world where the good suffer needlessly, where erotic love is more powerful
than divine, and where social and political systems are in a total state of collapse. As
everything descends into madness the truth emerges: some wounds are too deep to
heal; some broken families cannot be mended. —*Cassie Hay*

## Jean-Christophe Valtat
## 03
*Translated by Mitzi Angel; Farrar Strauss and Giroux, New York, 2010*
In a single-paragraph novella-sized rant a French teenage boy enumerates his reasons for loving a mentally retarded girl who waits at the bus stop across from his own. *03* sucks us into a perpetual motion swirl of logic; the protagonist is both brutality honest and aware of his own hypocrisies, and simultaneously uses the honesty as a veil to ignore the hypocrisies. Contemplating the nature of childhood, intelligence and delay, he loves the girl not because she would be an easy 'catch', but rather because of what she reflects about him, and the secret beauty she possesses that he believes only he can see. —*JS*


## Judy Rowe Michaels
## Reviewing the Skull
*WordTech Editions, Cincinnati, OH, 2010*
The plaintive, beautifully cadenced poems in Judy Rowe Michaels's *Reviewing the Skull* direct our attention to the most essential questions about the world we inhabit: How best to live with the knowledge of one's own mortality? Should we praise the fleeting character of our lives? Is it ever possible to seek refuge in the body? Michaels' poems are as finely crafted as they are ambitious, particularly as she uses form to illuminate and complicate the intense philosophical discussions offered in each piece. Just as the poet does not claim to resolve these longstanding debates, her stylistic choices allow myriad possible readings of the text to exist within the same narrative space. —*Kristina Marie Darling*


## Brian Henry
## Wings without Words
*Salt Publishing, London, 2010*
Henry has given us a huge book in this small volume. Though, thematically, he sticks close to home (daughter-love, poet-love, house, and garden), the work is rangy in dynamic and form, the poems unsentimental and crisp, pensive and grounded. Two stand-outs: "Epithalamium," which opens "What was I / but a cell in motion / the occasional collision," and closes exquisitely with "When I see I / there are two there," and the fifteen-page, single-stanza somewhat-Ashberian (and even better than

wholly-Ashberian) "Where We Stand Now," with its embedded refrain that surprises every time. A fabulous sixth collection by a fascinating writer. —*Renée Ashley*

## Mela Hartwig
## Am I a Redundant Human Being?

*Translated by Kerri Pierce; Dalkey Archives, Champaign, IL, 2010*

For pathologically insecure Luise, life is a series of funhouse mirrors, grotesquely skewing her self-image from moment to moment. This leads to ambitions in love and work that lose all sense of proportion: she'll be best in her class; no, she'll become a famous actress; no, she'll be the best secretary in the world; and so on. She loses job after job for mild incompetence, and fares little better in love, immediately deserted by her first lover (not an insignificant event in WWI-era Germany). But is she a redundant human being? Or . . . is the histrionic self-hatred on display really the sadomasochist's paradoxical reward? Even the least indulgent readers will recognize their inner narcissist in this fascinating tale of self-obsession. —*Anne McPeak*

## January Gill O'Neil
## Underlife

*CavanKerry Press, Fort Lee, NJ, 2009*

Towards the beginning of January Gill O'Neil's *Underlife* there is a masterpiece called "Night Work," a breathtaking meditation on the author's mother's shift as a nurse monitoring premature babies, and from there onward *Underlife* is filled with masterful poems with metaphysical sinew and a deliciously electric sense of presence. The later sections bring the reader through a succession of visions and experience that are emotionally powerful, and announce the arrival of a great talent. —*John King*

## Srečko Kosovel
## Look Back, Look Ahead: The Selected Poems of Srečko Kosovel

*Translated by Ana Jelnikar and Barbara Siegel Carlson;*
*Ugly Duckling Presse, New York, 2010*

There is a bold earnestness to Kosovel's poems in *Look Back, Look Ahead* that seems simultaneously like a bygone time and the expressions of an effusive, eccentric friend.

Collectively, the poems defy categorization. Over here he sounds like the eighth century Taosit poet Wang Wei, but on the next page he sounds like what Kafka might have been like as a poet. You might even make the association to Baudelaire's prose poems. The breadth of Kosovel's poetic registers is only matched by the resourcefulness of his prolific, thrilling insights. —*JK*

## Kim Dana Kupperman
### I Just Lately Started Buying Wings: Missives from the Other Side of Silence
*Graywolf Press, New York, 2010*

One of the essays in Kim Dana Kupperman's *I Just Lately Started Buying Wings* begins: "My mother is pregnant with me in my best memories of her." But her love for her mother, and her mother's love for her, is much more complex than that powerhouse of a sentence implies. And it is this combination of unrelenting honestly and precise poetics, that forces us into uncomfortable and kind of true places. In fact, there is not a moment when Kupperman's truths—her loves, her disappointments, her desires— are not laid out on the table for the reader's immediate emotional benefit. We lap up her delicious prose, her dorky love of syntax, her brilliant connections. —*JS*

## Barbara Henning
### Cities and Memory
*Chax Press, Tucson, AZ, 2010*

As a child living outside Detroit, Barbara Henning's prose poems tell us, she watches cars rush by and wonders, "Where are they going?" Then she, herself, goes—from Detroit to New York, India, Russia, California, Tucson—her path interwoven with the complex human connections she makes as kin and friend. In one magical poem, "we" walk through her childhood home where "a man with very large ears, sound asleep," half wakes up. She could be a cohort of one of her favorite writers, Roberto Bolaño; they are both observers of new worlds and old. —*Phyllis Wat*

# Matthew Gagnon
# Keith Waldrop's Woven Light: A Review of *Several Gravities*

Last fall, just as the warmer weather was getting increasingly stingy and the daylight slowly beginning to recalibrate itself at the end of the day, I read Keith Waldrop's fictional memoir, *Light While There Is Light: An American History*. Now, I am struck by its opening passages as they correspond to his wonderfully essential new project, *Several Gravities,* an intrepid merge of art and poetry. *Light* begins: "I've read many stories of revenants and apparitions, but my ghosts merely disappear. I never see them. They haunt me by not being there, by the table where no one eats, the empty window that lets the sun in without a shadow." Waldrop's account of reading substantially raises the stakes for how I might encounter and salvage a province of being. Every existence must by necessity face its negative quantity. Or must it? Maybe Waldrop is suggesting that it is the negative whence we begin, the scraps that must be assembled into order—or the semblance of order.

It is rare that a book is bound with such mystery and illumination, whose structure—a fusion of mixed media collages and assemblages and poem fragments— offers an alternative route to understanding Waldrop's world. For years, his exemplary work in poetry and translation, and its dissemination through Burning Deck Press, which he co-founded some forty-eight years ago with his wife, Rosemarie Waldrop, has contributed to and enlarged the poetic field of the possible. By now, Waldrop is extremely important, both in the flourishing community of writers and artists that circulate around his haven in Providence, Rhode Island, and to the more

Edited by Robert Seydel, Siglio, Los Angeles, 2009.

expanded transnational sensibility that he has championed by bringing modern and contemporary French poets into conversation with the American grain through translation.

I do not often find *astonishment* in a text. And even more rare is that a book beautifully constructs a counterpoint between two mediums, forcing them to speak in a new space where what is explored is the gap between the visible and unseen: the aura of location and dislocation. The collages and the poetry do not propose a commentary on each other, but provide a passageway without map or instruction. In other words, the suggestive/suggested gaze rather than directed interpretation is paramount. For me, *Several Gravities* signals a partial dreamscape, a mythologer's cartographic salvaging, an antiquity without a past. Its contents cut into and reconfigure the real.

Formally, the appearance and architecture of *Several Gravities,* the object, is exquisite. In this limited edition, Siglio Press lovingly reproduces portions of Waldrop's collages both on the front and back cover, while in the interior, a resonant form is found for Waldrop's hybrid work, reproducing the collages with such clarity. It announces itself as an event, an opening to a sublime experience. Waldrop's work as poet, translator, and visual artist seems to inhabit the space in between, say, the Doric columns at the Parthenon and the vision of Kurt Schwitters's collages and Joseph Cornell's boxes.

What's most immediate about Waldrop's collages is that they are built with anything from torn snatches of paper to images mined from newspapers and comic books to old stamps and maps. Collages by nature emphasize their form. In one collage you will see a burning candelabra juxtaposed with what appears to be the silhouette of someone's face. In another, an image of a marble staircase leads to an entrance that surrealistically becomes a passage into a body's lower half. The pieces are variously busy, but not in a manner that crowds the surface with surplus material. They build up to a palimpsest that reaches toward a contradictory but elevated surface; in short, Waldrop's art "encourages abstraction." The random flux of image overlapping image asks the viewer to consider how dialogue might be created or suggested.

I am tempted to read Waldrop's remark that he has "no sky" in his collages as an invocation of a larger order and formal feature of his visual work. We are confronted with his practice of "eliminating space." When comparing his visual work to that of Kurt Schwitters, Waldrop writes that he brings together "elements in a way [Schwitters] does not. Thus, when working with paper, my elements are usually torn rather than cut. A large proportion of the elements touch one or another edge, suggesting incompletion." In this sense, undefined outlines perform an intricate space whose details must by read in their accumulation. For instance, how am I to make sense of a collage that generates a surface reliant on color, scratchings, found images, and occasional scraps of text? There is no easy answer. And perhaps there shouldn't be one. Waldrop's collages seem marked by a refusal to descend into stabilizing or locating objects.

Waldrop's mixed-media collages collapse under his present hand into a form without a form. As Seydel says in his essay "Imagination's Artifacts," "Form even more than figure is always 'flying away' in a Waldrop collage." In the new book, one of my favorite collages, "Untitled [Archway]," whose surface is busy with the overlaying of paper materials, vein-like black markings, and the semblance of an archway fading into the black beyond is set adjacent to an excerpt of Waldrop's 1987 poem, "Water Marks":

> Woven, the net, without
> really thinking—is
> the process
> blind? It is all
> edge, all surface. If you
> want to be
> taken in,
> go deep. A
> random or a systematic mistake
> "explains" everything, whereas
> all he wants to know lies
> spread to the horizon,
> unpronounceable.

Waldrop's poem, in its rapidly disintegrating logic and truncated phrasing, is provocative for its rhetorical questioning about process, but also its terminology of making. Can the figurations of making cross boundaries of form and medium? Waldrop's answer is, *Of course*. The poem is beyond commentary on the process of making. It suggests a course for composition but resists the decrees of an artist becoming surefooted in his process. As Waldrop would have it, I am invited to "Go deep" while encountering a horizon that is "unpronounceable."

What is striking about Waldrop's formal engagements in *Several Gravities* is his insistent compositional techniques. For Waldrop, there seems to be no prefigured conception of the thing to be created. Not that Waldrop's collages are a jumbled mess of randomness or chance procedures; their surfaces are articulate and expressive, while occasionally disembodied and formally claustrophobic. But this is the strength of his labor: the immediacy of juxtaposed elements and images configured "As through a fixed window, he finds a kind of space, the vis- / ible world foreshortened."

*Several Gravities* permits one to discover, in Waldrop's words, a "spectacle without entrance." It's also a book where Waldrop materializes an elsewhere of making: "Quotations / drop from the air, forms / of hieroglyphic." The evocation of this elsewhere or outside as source material seems to be a perfect meditation on how we might consider our relationships among words and things, and moreover, how to refigure what is plucked from a source so that it can breathe as it's given a new life. But in this new life, something is metamorphosed, changed, transfigured. This level of art is fundamentally moving and fluid. In one of Waldrop's prose poems he writes, "random details proportion themselves, heighten into tone. Any picture is another world, and suggests a *whole* world." Instead of attempting to render a work of art as useless unless it can function as markedly relatable, Waldrop places me just at the edge where meaning and the possibilities for meaning emerge. This can make for a tenuous negotiation. But by considering Waldrop's sources, whether textual or material, which contain their own ghosts there is intrigue and melancholy inherent in their rebirth on canvas or page.

In his essay, "A Matter of Collage," which opens *Several Gravities*, Waldrop negotiates the lineaments of collage and quotation: "A quote keeps something of its own character and is read (or, in a painting, seen) as transcribed from elsewhere. A collage element, losing its substance, becomes part of a new texture and former connections may be lost completely." What provides a bridge between quotation and collage is that *elsewhere* haunting the visual or textual mark. Thinking through this elsewhere, trying to come to terms with its troubled surface and the dislocation of bringing disparate textual sources or images into a new relation, is the cost of arriving at a more fertile ground.

His poems, like the collages, are sometimes derivative. They work quietly to preserve multiple voices and sources, while fanning outward to express a conglomeration of tones that perhaps captures the ambiance of his work in collage. In the poem, "Poem From Memory," Waldrop writes: "I / live within / acceptable / tolerances. At the / intersection of innumerable / fantasies. Irreconcilables / point me to / my orient." There is an abounding wildness defying attempts to find unity in the merging of textural and textual ingredients corresponding to Waldrop's visual work. It is a welcome challenge. I love the suggestibility of the book's title, which challenges the prospect of a singular gravity to start out from, like "An unfolding, from where it is all contained." Instead of being inscribed within a singular, familiar gravity, I encounter *Several Gravities* as an incipient community of works. Instead of looking for a governing thread or useful binary between forms, my expectations must be put to sea. My encounter must be a beginning.

Artistic engagement is always irreducible to a set of prescriptive models of process and creation. But it is within the act of creating a work of art that something else is *de-created*. This is a better way to think of Waldrop's compositions: the greater evolving and devolving confluency of mind and source, exercising imagination's unsettled and numerous directions. In short, this is not a book for the faint of heart. Waldrop is not interested in a laissez-faire modality, which resists intervention from where the mind chooses to wander. The composite textuality of these poems summons the negational qualities of saying "This is the house I did not build." And one might wonder: what is being built after all? But finding this balance between the built and unbuilt in *Several Gravities* suggests that Waldrop's doppelganger might be a glyph-maker, making fragmentation collect around a space while allowing it to hold a surplus of possibilities. That's just what this publication conjures for me: an opportunity to be restlessly pitched back and forth in the tempest of receptivity.

The lack of a complete chronological documentation for these untitled collages casts aside the arc of artistic progression so that we are free to remain in flight from one collage to the next, while flight is briefly postponed so that we can engage with the text of Waldrop's excerpted poems. While transitioning between the visual and textual, we are permitted to take on a kind of Emersonian creative reading: "One must be an inventor," wrote Emerson, "to read well." This sensibility accounts for the challenge inherent in "reading" Waldrop's project. As Seydel remarks, when speaking of the lineage of poet-artists, this endeavor is "a kind of dance that rejects differences in medium, intention, and feeling. What is visible in the opening they provide is a specific freedom, of conception and inspiration, of imagination as larger than training or medium."

I am tempted to say that one of the most illuminating moments of traveling through *Several Gravities* is the recognition that order is illusory. It's not that Waldrop fails in constructing the blueprints for order, but that he is a more likely candidate to wander through the clouds of dust, the junctions and interstices, the antiquary and contemporary, the luminous and darkled. But even within these abstract entities or qualities, Waldrop masterfully brings a kind of form. The visual and textual bear witness to and absorb their sources, giving birth to the counterpart of what's found.

# Contributors

**R.A. Allen** ("Monday Burning" 125) lives in Memphis. His fiction and poetry have appeared or are forthcoming in *The Los Angeles Review*, *JMWW*, *The New York Quarterly*, *Pear Noir!*, *Boston Literary Magazine*, *The Recusant* (UK), *Word Riot*, *Underground Voices*, *PANK*, and others. Selected for Houghton Mifflin's Best American Mystery Stories 2010. Nominated by *LITnIMAGE* for Dzanc Books' Best of the Web 2010.

**Renée Ashley** (Books 189, 205) is the poetry editor of *The Literary Review*.

**Ann Beman** (Books 181) is *The Los Angeles Review*'s nonfiction editor and lives with her husband and two whatchamaterriers on California's Kern River. After taking a recent swiftwater rescue course, she knows how it must feel to sleep in a moving cement mixer.

**Jason Lee Brown** ("Big Cowboy" 35) teaches at Eastern Illinois University and is co-series editor of *New Stories from the Midwest*. He is finishing a novel.

Canadian writer **Jeff Bursey** (Books 204) has written reviews and articles for journals in Canada, the United Kingdom, and the United States. His first book, *Verbatim: A Novel*, will be released in the fall of 2010.

**M. Eileen Cronin** ("The Hanger Artificial Limb Company" 51). Her publications include *Third Coast*, *Bellevue*, *G.W.* and *Coe* reviews, the *Washington Post*, and one forthcoming in *Slice*. She won the Washington Writing Prize, was a finalist in the Faulkner-Wisdom, was nominated for a Pushcart, and is on the *Narrative* staff.

**Ruth Curry** (Books 196) is a writer living in Brooklyn.

**Weston Cutter** (poems 122) is from Minnesota, has poems forthcoming in the *Southern Review* and *Ploughshares*, and his first book of fiction, *You'd Be a Stranger, Too*, will be released this winter. He edits the blog Corduroy Books.

**Jim Daniels'** (poems 81) new and forthcoming collections include *Having a Little Talk with Capital P Poetry*; *From Milltown to Malltown*, a collaborative book with photographer Charlee Brodsky and writer Jane McCafferty; and *All of the Above*.

**Kristina Marie Darling** (Books 205) is the author of *Night Songs*, a full-length collection of poems available from Gold Wake Press.

**Lawrence-Minh Bùi Davis** ("Like Kissing Your Sister" 75). His work has appeared in *McSweeney's Quarterly Concern*, *The New York Quarterly*, *AGNI Online*, *The Louisville Review*, *Fiction International*, and *Pedestal Magazine*. He is a founding co-editor-in-chief of *The Asian American Literary Review*.

**Matthew Gagnon** (Books 208). His reviews and essays have appeared in *Jacket*, *The Poker*, *Word For/Word: A Journal of New Writing*, and *Octopus Magazine*. Poems are forthcoming in *The Nation*, *Colorado Review*, and *Model Homes*. He lives in Amherst with his wife.

**Eamon Grennan** (poems 68). His most recent poetry collections are *Still Life with Waterfall*, which won the Lenore Marshall Prize; *The Quick of It*; and *Matter of Fact*. He translated *Oedipus at Colonus* with Rachel Kitzinger. His new collection, *Out of Sight: New and Selected Poems*, is coming out this summer. He lives in Poughkeepsie, NY, and whenever he can in Renvyle, a peninsula in the west of Ireland. Each of his poems in this issue speaks of one of these places.

**Jody Handerson** (Books 199) has a widely varied background in the visual and performing arts. She currently applies her literary talent as a technical writer and editor for an environmental consulting company. She is a contributing editor to *The Literary Review*.

**Cassie Hay** (Books 204) is an essayist and filmmaker living in Jersey City. She is the writer/associate producer of *Gotham Girls Roller Derby*, produced for NYC Media.

**John King** (Books 206), literary rock star, has just wrapped up his MFA in creative writing from NYU after earning his PhD in English literature from Purdue. His fiction has appeared in *Painted Bride Quarterly*, *Turnrow*, *Pearl*, and *Gargoyle*. Watch the sky for his next move.

**Andrew McKay** (Books 194) is the director of advancement communications at Fairleigh Dickinson University, and volunteers as a poetry reader for *The Literary Review*. He is working on his first book, titled *Living Here*, which chronicles his family's triumph over poverty.

**Anne McPeak** (Books 206) is the managing editor of *A Public Space*. She lives in Brooklyn.

**M.A. Melnick** ("Obediently Yours" 15) received her MFA from Brooklyn College. Her stories have appeared in *Many Waters*, *Brooklyn Review*, *Contrary*, *Pindeldyboz*, *Eclipse*, and *Carve Magazine*. She is at work on a collection.

**Lina Meruane** ("False Steps" 144) was born in Chile and has authored one collection of short stories, *Las Infantas*, and three novels: *Postuma Cercada*, and *Fruta Podrida*. She has received grants from the Guggenheim Foundation and the NEA. She has lived in New York City since 2000.

**Peter E. Murphy** (poems 63) received a 2009 Poetry Fellowship from the NJ State Council on the Arts. He is the author of two books of poems, *Stubborn Child* and *Thorough and Efficient*.

**Benjamin Paloff** (poems 43) is the author of *The Politics*, a collection of poems, and has translated several books from Polish, including the forthcoming *Lodgings: Selected Poems of Andrzej Sosnowski*. The recipient of fellowships from the National Endowment for the Arts and the Fulbright Program, he teaches at the University of Michigan and is a poetry editor at *Boston Review*.

**Doug Ramspeck** (poems 135). His poetry collection, *Black Tupelo Country*, received the 2007 John Ciardi Prize for Poetry.

**J.D. Reid** (Books 203) is co-founder of Wide Array Press. He lives in Texas.

**Thomas Reiter** (poems 170). His most recent poetry book, *Catchment*, was published in 2009. He has received fellowships from the NEA and the NJ State Council on the Arts.

**James Richardson** (poems 9) His collection, *Interglacial*, was a finalist for the 2004 National Book Critics Circle Award. These aphorisms will appear in *By the Numbers*.

**Eli M. Rosenberg** ("So It Goes" 114) lives in Brooklyn. This is his first published work.

**Tomaž Šalamun** (poems 108) lives in Ljubljana, Slovenia and occasionally teaches in the US. His recent books translated into English are *Woods and Chalices*, *Poker*, and *There's the Hand and There's the Arid Chair*. His *Blue Tower* is forthcoming in Spring 2011.

**Jena Salon** (Books 203) is the books editor for *The Literary Review*.

**Norman Simon** ("ESPN" 87) is a retired professor of astrophysics. His stories have appeared in *Center*, *Hawai'i Pacific Review*, *The Massachusetts Review*, and *New South*. He has recently completed a novel, *Thoronet*.

**Michael Thomas Taren** (translator, poems 108). His translations of Tomaž Šalamun have appeared widely and and are forthcoming in the *Chicago Review*, *Public Space*, *Circumference*, and elsewhere. Taren's own book, *Puberty*, is a finalist in the *Fence* Poetry Series.

**Padma Thornlyre** (poems 151) resides in the canyon village of Kittredge, CO. His long poem, *Mavka*, in 51 parts, will appear in 2011, featuring cover art by Bryan Comber.

**Mariana Toscas** (poems 25) is a poet, artist, and marketing professional. She was born and raised in Chicago but can often be seen dreaming of and traveling to faraway places. She is a recent graduate of the Vermont College of Fine Arts MFA program where she learned to be an alchemist of trauma by channeling Goddess energy.

**Mike Valente** ("Solitude" 157) was writer-in-residence at the University of Notre Dame, where he earned an MFA. He also has a degree from Stanford University.

**Bernadette Walker** (translator, "False Steps" 144) is a freelance translator based in Brooklyn. Her work has been published in *BOMB Magazine*'s Literary Supplement, *First Proof*. She is currently translating Lina Meruane's *Las Infantas*, which contains the short story "False Steps."

**Phyllis Wat** (Books 207) is a poet with three books in print, most recently *The Influence of Paintings Hung in Bedrooms*. She is also publisher of Straw Gate Books, a poetry press.

**Scott Withiam** (poems 101) His work has recently appeared in *Agni, AGNI Online, Beloit Poetry Journal, Cimarron Review, Ploughshares,* and *Tar River Poetry Review*.

**Marion Wyce** (Books 185) has received an AWP Intro Journals Award in Fiction and had her work performed in the Interact Theatre Company's stage series Writing Aloud.

# Index to Volume 53 (2009–2010)

Volume 53 of *The Literary Review* consists of four numbers:

1. Fall (October 2009)    2. Winter (January 2010)
3. Spring (April 2010)    4. Summer (July 2010)

The issues of Volume 53 are paged separately beginning with page 1. The index is arranged alphabetically, using the following abbreviations:

ART  art and photography    B    books: essay/review
EDIT editorial              E    essay
F    fiction                INT  interview
P    poetry                 TR   translator

# TLR SUBSCRIBE TODAY!

☐ **ONE YEAR US $24**
**INTERNATIONAL $32**

☐ **TWO YEARS US $36**
**INTERNATIONAL $45**

SELECT BACK ISSUES:

☐ **THERAPY!** QUANTITY: ___
☐ **MACHISMO** QUANTITY: ___
☐ **HOW TO READ MUSIC** QUANTITY: ___

_____

NAME

_____

ADDRESS

_____

CITY/STATE/ZIP                          COUNTRY

_____

EMAIL

☐ CHECK ENCLOSED          CHARGE MY CREDIT CARD: ☐ VISA  ☐ MC  ☐ AMEX

_____

CARD NUMBER                          EXPIRATION DATE

_____

SIGNATURE

I'D LIKE TO SUPPORT LITERATURE. PLEASE ADD A TAX-DEDUCTIBLE CONTRIBUTION OF $_____ TO MY ORDER.

Send completed form to: *The Literary Review*, 285 Madison Avenue, Madison, NJ 07940 USA
Telephone: (973) 443-8564  Fax: (973) 443-8364  Email: info@theliteraryreview.org  Web: theliteraryreview.org

# 2009–2010
# Charles Angoff Awards

We are pleased to announce the twenty-sixth annual Charles Angoff Awards for outstanding contributions during a volume year.

The winners for Volume 53 are:

## POETRY
### Catherine Doty
(The First Time I Was Told To Fuck Myself;
Breathing Under Water; Behind Bars; Sweet Ants; Fall 2009)

*Finalists*: Scott Withiam (Summer 2010) and Mariana Toscas (Summer 2010)

## FICTION
### Percival Everett
("Confluence," Spring 2010)

*Finalists*: Kelly Luce (Spring 2010) and Robert Repino (Fall 2009)

This cash award, named in honor of *The Literary Review*'s editor from 1957–1976, is supported by family, friends, and colleagues of the late Charles Angoff. It recognizes his initiative in helping to found *The Literary Review*, his encouragement of excellence in writing, and his own achievements as a poet, essayist, and novelist.